Introducing Swift

Contents

Chapter 1: Getting Started

In case you haven't heard, Apple just introduced a new language for iOS and OSX developers called Swift. It has come to light that Swift was in the works since 2010, which is 2 years after the first SDK was released. Apple saw the limitations of Objective-C which is almost 30 years old and decided it was time for a change. However, in true Apple fashion, they did not want to release a half-baked language. They realized that no matter the drawbacks of Objective-C, they could still push the envelope with it, and so they did.

When talking about Swift, Apple refers to three key considerations: Safe, Modern and Powerful. It lives up to all those three things. Outlined below are some of the very basics you need to get up and running with Swift. If you already know a programming language, then you will see a lot of similarities with other modern languages. You might even wonder why they had to invent a whole new language, but that is discussion for another blog post.

1.1 Installing the Tools

Firstly, you will have to download and install Xcode 6. Once you have installed it, open it up and select File from the menu -> New -> Select Source on the left under either iOS or OSX -> Playground. Give your playground a name and you are ready to get started.

Alternatively, you could use the REPL (Read Evaluate Print Loop) from the terminal.

Steps

Instructions to run from the terminal:

1. Open up terminal

2. If you have two or more versions of Xcode installed then you will need to select Xcode 6 as your default version. If you are only running Xcode 6 then skip ahead to step 3. If you are only running Xcode 6 then skip ahead to step 3, otherwise go ahead and run the following line:

sudo xcode-select -s /Applications/Xcode6-Beta.app/Contents/Developer/

At the time of writing this post beta version of Xcode 6 was named "Xcode6-Beta". Please check your app name in the "Applications" folder to write out the appropriate path when using xcode-select.

3. To start the REPL type:

 xcrun swift

1.2 Creating Your First Cocoa App

To start experimenting with accessing Cocoa frameworks in Swift, create a Swift-based app from one of the Xcode templates.

To create a Swift project in Xcode

1. Choose File > New > Project > (iOS or OS X) > Application > your template of choice.

2. Click the Language pop-up menu and choose Swift.

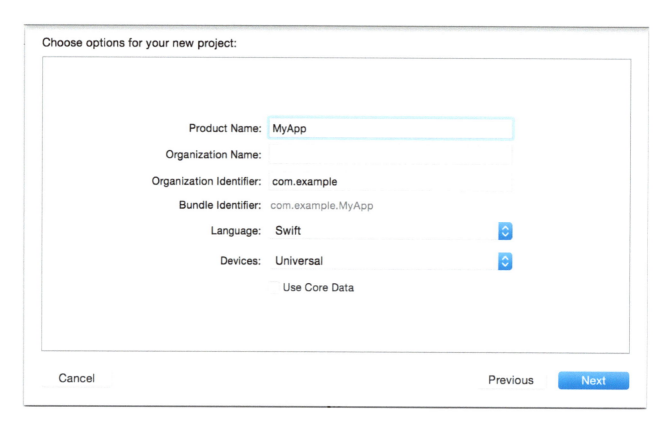

A Swift project's structure is nearly identical to an Objective-C project, with one important distinction: Swift has no header files. There is no explicit delineation between the implementation and the interface, so all the information about a particular class resides in a single .swift file.

From here, you can start experimenting by writing Swift code in the app delegate, or you can create a new Swift class file by choosing File > New > File > (iOS or OS X) > Source > Swift.

Understanding the Swift Import Process

After you have your Xcode project set up, you can import any framework from the Cocoa platform to start working with Objective-C from Swift.

Any Objective-C framework (or C library) that's accessible as a module can be imported directly into Swift. This includes all of the Objective-C system frameworks—such as Foundation, UIKit, and SpriteKit—as well as common C libraries supplied with the system. For example, to import Foundation, simply add this import statement to the top of the Swift file you're working in:

SWIFT

import Foundation

This import makes all of the Foundation APIs—including NSDate, NSURL, NSMutableData, and all of their methods, properties, and categories—directly available in Swift.

The import process is straightforward. Objective-C frameworks vend APIs in header files. In Swift, those header files are compiled down to Objective-C modules, which are then imported into Swift as Swift APIs. The importing determines how functions, classes, methods, and types declared in Objective-C code appear in Swift. For functions and methods, this process affects the types of their arguments and return values. For types, the process of importing can do the following things:

- Remap certain Objective-C types to their equivalents in Swift, like id to AnyObject

- Remap certain Objective-C core types to their alternatives in Swift,

  like NSString to String

- Remap certain Objective-C concepts to matching concepts in Swift, like pointers to

  optionals

In Interoperability, you'll learn more about these mappings and about how to leverage them in your Swift code.

The model for importing Swift into Objective-C is similar to the one used for importing Objective-C into Swift. Swift vends its APIs—such as from a framework—as Swift modules. Alongside these Swift modules are generated Objective-C headers. These headers vend the APIs that can be mapped back to Objective-C. Some Swift APIs do not map back to Objective-C because they leverage language features that are not available in Objective-C. For more information on using Swift in Objective-C, see Swift and Objective-C in the Same Project.

1.3 Understanding Cocoa and Swift

Swift is designed to provide seamless compatibility with Cocoa and Objective-C. You can use Objective-C APIs (ranging from system frameworks to your own custom code) in Swift, and you can use Swift APIs in Objective-C. This compatibility makes Swift an easy, convenient, and powerful tool to integrate into your Cocoa app development workflow.

This guide covers three important aspects of this compatibility that you can use to your advantage when developing Cocoa apps:

- *Interoperability* lets you interface between Swift and Objective-C code, allowing you to use Swift classes in Objective-C and to take advantage of familiar Cocoa classes, patterns, and practices when writing Swift code.

- *Mix and match* allows you to create mixed-language apps containing both Swift and Objective-C files that can communicate with each other.

- *Migration* from existing Objective-C code to Swift is made easy with interoperability and mix and match, making it possible to replace parts of your Objective-C apps with the latest Swift features.

Before you get started learning about these features, you need a basic understanding of how to set up a Swift environment in which you can access Cocoa system frameworks

Chapter 2: Introduction to Swift

2.1 Creating a Playground

To get started developing your app, you create a new Xcode project.

To create a new project

1. Launch Xcode (located in the Applications folder).

If you've never created or opened a project in Xcode before, you should see a Welcome to Xcode window similar to this:

If you've created or opened a project in Xcode before, you might see a project window instead of the Welcome to Xcode window.

2. In the Welcome to Xcode window, click "Create a new Xcode project" (or choose File > New > Project).

Xcode opens a new window and displays a dialog in which you choose a template. Xcode includes several built-in app templates that you can use to develop common styles of Mac apps.

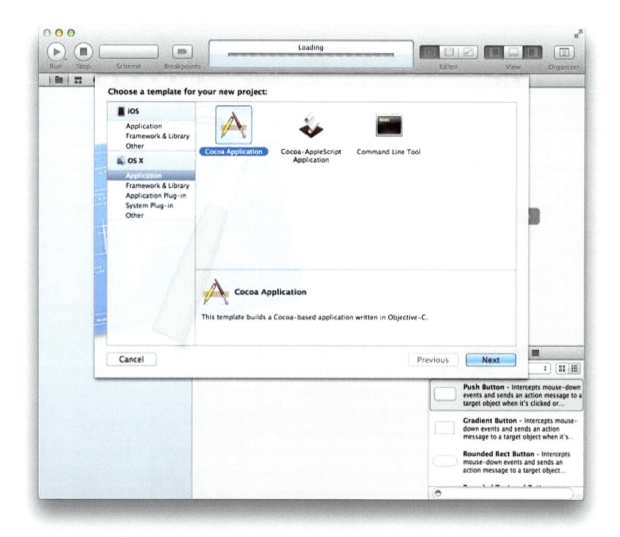

3. In the OS X section to the left of the dialog, select Application.

4. In the main area of the dialog, select Cocoa Application and click Next.

A new dialog appears that prompts you to name your app and choose additional options for your project.

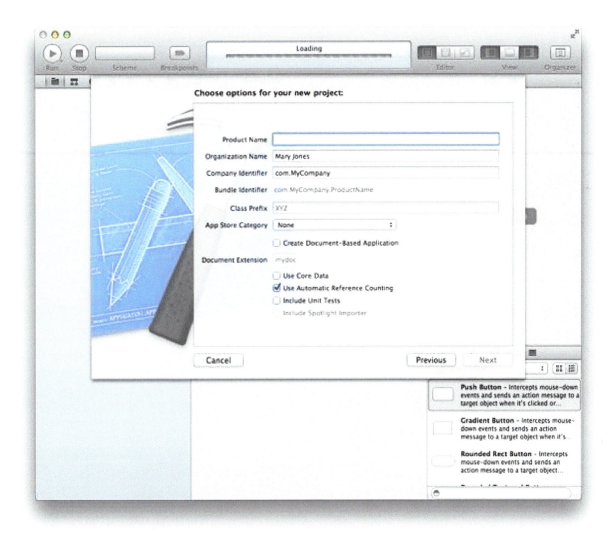

5. Choose the following options:

- In the Product Name field, type `TrackMix`.

- In the Company Identifier field, type the identifier for your company,

  or `com.MyCompany`.

- In the App Store Category pop-up, choose None.

Note: Xcode uses the product name you entered to name your project and the app. To keep things simple, this tutorial assumes that you named your product TrackMix and did not specify a class prefix value. (The prefix is used to create unique class names for your app that won't conflict with classes in other frameworks.) The organization name property that appears in this dialog is not used in this tutorial.

6. Make sure that the Use Automatic Reference Counting option is selected and that the Create Document-Based Application (appears above Document Extension), Use Core Data, and Include Unit Tests options are unselected.

7. Click Next.

Another dialog appears that allows you to specify where to save your project.

8. Specify a location for your project (make sure that the Source Control option is unselected) and then click Create.

Xcode opens your new project in a window (called the workspace window), which should look similar to this:

Take a few moments to familiarize yourself with the workspace window that Xcode opens for you. You'll use the buttons and areas identified in the window below throughout the rest of this tutorial.

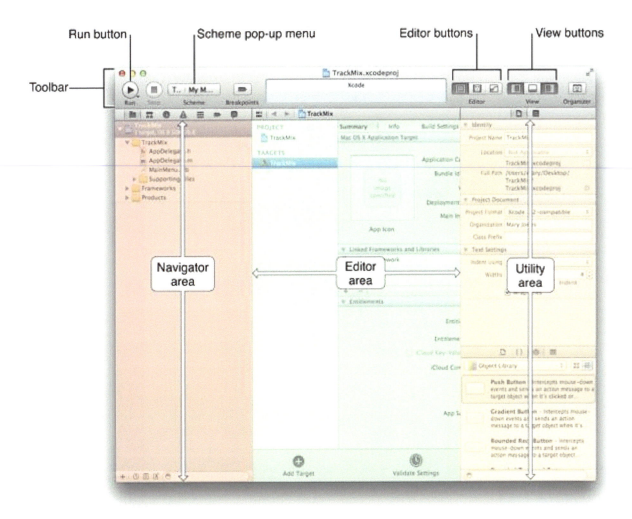

If the utilities area in your workspace window is already open (as it is in the window shown above), you can close it for now because you won't need it until later in the tutorial. The rightmost View button controls the utilities area. When the utilities area is visible, the button looks like this:

If necessary, click the rightmost View button to close the utilities area.

Even though you haven't yet written any code, you can build and run your app in Xcode.

To build and test the app

1. Click the Run button in the Xcode toolbar (or choose Product > Run).

If a dialog appears asking whether Xcode should enable developer mode on this Mac, click Disable.

Xcode should build your project and launch the app. When your app starts up, it should have a standard menu bar and display a single window.

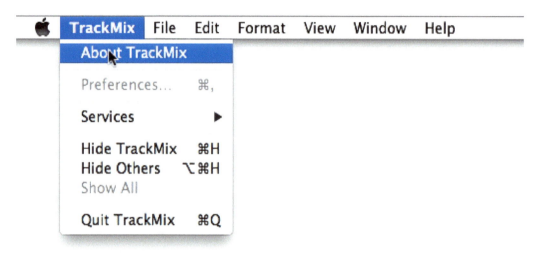

2. Test the app.

You can move and resize the window. However, if you close the window, there is no way to get it back. You should also find that menus display when you click them, and if you choose TrackMix > About TrackMix, an About window is displayed.

3. Quit the app by choosing TrackMix > Quit TrackMix.

Don't mistakenly choose the Quit command in Xcode, or you'll quit Xcode. You can also click the Stop button in Xcode.

Right now, your app is not very interesting: it simply displays a blank window. To understand where the blank window comes from, you need to learn about the objects in your code and how they work together to start the app.

2.1 Creating variables and constants

Variables

As with every programming language you have variables which allow you to store data. To declare a variable you have to use the keyword var.

var greeting: String = "Hello World"

The above code instructs the system that you want to create a variable named greeting which is of typeString and it will contain the text, "Hello World".

Swift is smart enough to infer that if you are assigning a string to a variable and in fact that variable will be of type string. So you need not explicitly specify the type as in the above example. A better and common way of writing the above example would be:

var greeting = "Hello World" // Inferred type String

Variables can be modified once created so we could add another line and change our greeting to something else.

var greeting = "Hello World" // Inferred type String

greeting = "Hello Swift"

While writing an application there are many instances where you don't want to change a variable once it has been initialized. Apple has always had two variants of types mutable and immutable. Mutable meaning the variable can be modified and immutable that it cannot be modified. They prefer immutability by default which means that the values aren't going to change and it makes your app faster and safer in a multi-threaded environment. To create an immutable variable you need to use the keyword let.

If we change our greeting example to use let instead of var then the second line will give us a compiler error because we cannot modify greeting.

let greeting = "Hello World"

greeting = "Hello Swift" //Compiler error

Lets take another example so you understand why and when to use let.

let languageName: String = "Swift"

var version: Double = 1.0

let introduced: Int = 2014

let isAwesome: Bool = true

The above example not only shows us the various types that are available in Swift but it also shows us that the reason to use let. Aside from the version number of the Swift language everything else remains constants. You might argue that isAwesome is debatable but I'll let you reach that conclusion once you reach the end of this post.

Since the type is inferred we should simply write:

let languageName = "Swift" // inferred as String

var version = 1.0 // inferred as Double

let introduced = 2014 // inferred as Int

let isAwesome = true // inferred as Bool

Strings

In our above example we have been writing the String type. Lets see how we can concatenate two strings by using the + operator.

let title = "An Absolute Beginners Guide to Swift"

let review = "Is Awesome!"

let description = title + " - " + review

// description = "An Absolute Beginners Guide to Swift - Is Awesome!"

Strings have a powerful string interpolation feature where it's easy to use variables to create a strings.

let datePublished = "June 9th, 2014"

let postMeta = "Blog Post published on: \(datePublished)"

// postMeta = "Blog Post published on: June 9th, 2014"

In all the above examples, I have been using the keyword let which means you cannot modify the string once it has been created. However, if you do need to modify the string then simply use the keyword var.

Other Types

Besides strings you have Int for whole numbers. Double and Float for floating-point numbers and Boolfor boolean values such as: true of false. These types are inferred just as a string so you need not explicitly specify them when creating a variable.

A Float and Double vary in precision and how large of a number you can store.

- Float: represents a 32-bit floating-point number and the precision of Float can be as little as 6 decimal digits.
- Double: represents a 64-bit floating point number and has a precision of at least 15 decimal digits.

By default when you write a floating-point number it is inferred as a Double.

var version = 1.0 // inferred as Double

You can explicitly specify a Float.

var version: Float = 1.0

2.3 Creating Arrays And Dictionaries

Array

Collections come in two varieties. Firstly, an array which is a collection of data items which can be accessed via an index beginning with 0.

var cardNames: [String] = ["Jack", "Queen", "King"]

// Swift can infer [String] so we can also write it as:

var cardNames = ["Jack", "Queen", "King"] // inferred as [String]

You can create two types of arrays: an array of a single type or an array with multiple types. Swift is keen on being safe so it prefers the former but can accommodate the later with generic types. The example above is an array of strings which means that it is a single type array.

To access an item from the array you need to use the subscript:

println(cardNames[0])

Note: we used a function above called println which will print the value "Jack" to the console and then add a new line.

Modifying An Array

Lets create a new array that contains a todo list.

var todo = ["Write Blog","Return Call"]

Make sure that you use the keyword var so that we can modify our array.

To add another item to our todo array we use the '+=' operator:

todo += "Get Grocery"

To add multiple items to our todo array we simply append an array:

todo += ["Send email", "Pickup Laundry"]

To replace an existing item in the array simply subscript that item and provide a new value:

todo[0] = "Proofread Blog Post"

To replace an entire range of items:

todo[2..<5] = ["Pickup Laundry","Get Grocery", "Cook Dinner"]

Dictionary

The other collection type is a Dictionary which is similar to a Hash Table in other programming languages. A dictionary allows you to store key-value pairs and access the value by providing the key.

For example, we can specify our cards by providing their keys and subsequent values.

var cards = ["Jack" : 11, "Queen" : 12, "King" : 13]

Above we have specified the card names as the keys and their corresponding numerical value. Keys are not restricted to the String type, they can be of any type and so can the values.

Modifying A Dictionary

What if we wanted to add an "ace" to our cards dictionary? All we have to do is use the key as a subscript and assign it a value. Note: cards is defined as a var which means it can be modified.

cards["ace"] = 15

We made a mistake and want to change the value of "ace". Once again just use the key as the subscript and assign it a new value.

cards["ace"] = 1

To retrieve a value from the dictionary

println(cards["ace"])

2.4 Using Loops and Conditional Statements

Control Flow

Looping

What it good is a collection if you cannot loop over it? Swift provides while, do-while,for and for-inloops. Lets take a look at each one of them.

The easiest one of them is the while loop which states while something is true execute a block of code. It stops execution when that condition turns to false.

```
while !complete {

        println("Downloading...")

}
```

Note: the exclamation mark before the variable complete denotes not and is read as "not complete".

Likewise, you have the do-while loop which ensures that your block of code is executed at least once.

```
var message = "Starting to download"

do {

        println(message)

        message = "Downloading.."

} while !complete
```

Subsequent calls to the println statement will print "Downloading.."

You have the regular for loop where you can specify a number and increment that number to a certain value:

```
for var i = 1; i < cardNames.count; ++i {

        println(cardNames[i])

}
```

Or you can simply use the for-in variant where it creates a temporary variable and assigns it a value while iterating over the array.

```
for cardName in cardNames {

        println(cardName)

}
```

The above code will print out all the card names in the array. We can also use a range. A range of values is denoted by two dots or three dots.

For example:

- 1...10 – is a range of numbers from 1 to 10. The three dots are known as a closed range because the upper limit is inclusive.
- 1..<10 – is a range of numbers from 1 to 9. The two dots with a lesser-than sign is known as a half-closed range because the upper limit is non-inclusive.

Lets print out the 2 times table using for-in with a range:

```
for number in 1...10 {

        println("\(number) times 2 is \(number*2)")

}
```

We can also iterate over the cards dictionary to print out both the key and the value:

```
for (cardName, cardValue) in cards {

        println("\(cardName) = \(cardValue)")

}
```

IF STATEMENTS

To control the flow of our code we Ofcourse have an if statement.

```
if cardValue == 11 {
```

```
        println("Jack")

} else if cardValue == 12 {

        println("Queen")

} else {

        println("Not found")

}
```

Note: The if syntax can have parenthesis but they are optional. However, the braces {} are mandatory unlike other languages.

Switch Statement

The switch statement in Swift is very versatile and has a lot of features. Some basic rules about the switch statement:

- It doesn't require a break statement after each case statement
- The switch is not limited to integer values. You can match against any values such as: String, Int,Double or any object for that matter.
- The switch statement must match against every value possible if not you must have a default case which makes your code safer. If you don't provide a case for every value or a default then you will get a compiler error saying: "switch must be exhaustive".

```
switch cardValue {

        case 11:

                println("Jack")

        case 12:

                println("Queen")

        default:

                println("Not found")
```

}

Lets say you have a distance variable and you are trying to print a message based on distance. You can use multiple values for each case statement:

```
switch distance {

    case 0:

        println("not a valid distance")

    case 1,2,3,4,5:

        println("near")

    case 6,7,8,9,10:

        println("far")

    default:

        println("too far")

}
```

There are times when even multiple values are limiting. For those instances you can use ranges. What if any distance greater than 10 and less than 100 was considered far?

```
switch distance {

    case 0:

        println("not a valid distance")


    case 1..10:

        println("near")


    case 10..100 :

        println("far")
```

```
        default:

            println("too far")


}
```

Can you guess what the above code will print?

Swift: Beginner to Intermediate

Chapter 3: Core Cocoa Skills

Cocoa is a programming language which is what native Mac applications are written in. It is based on Objective C, which is in turn based on C. It is object-oriented. Objective C can be compiled to run on any platform, but Cocoa contains frameworks which are only designed to run on the Mac.

3.1 Introduction to Xcode

XCode is a Mac application which provides a programming environment (editor, documentation, project manager, debugger and compiler) for writing scripts and applications. It is especially suited for writing programs in C, C++, Objective C, Cocoa, Ruby and Python. XCode is installed on all the CoMPLEX computers and can also be downloaded for free from the Mac Dev Center after you sign up for a free account.

3.2 Using Model-View-Controller (MVC)

Set up the Interface

In Xcode, Create a new single-view Swift project. Call it PizzaDemo2. Go into the storyboard. On the bottom center of the storyboard, you will find the class sizes button labeled w:Any h:Any. Click the button and change the class size to Compact Width Any Height:

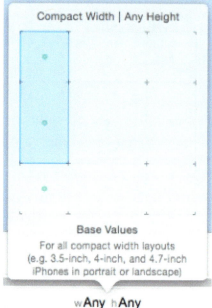

To the storyboard add a label, two buttons, and a segmented control. Make one of the buttons with a red background and white lettering, make the title of the button readClear. Set the second button to a white foreground lettering and a blue background, but don't set a title yet. Make the Segmented control four segments with Cheese, Sausage, Pepperoni,and Veggie. Your layout should look something like this:

Initial Layout in interface Builder

I did not use constraints here, but if you want to you certainly can.

Set Up the View Controller

Open the assistant editor, and control drag the controls to make the following IBOutlets and IBActions. Note in the comments which one is the red and which one is the blue button. Remember from last time to physically change from an outlet to an action for the buttons and the segmented controls. Interface builder picks an outlet by default.

1   @IBOutlet var resultsDisplayLabel : UILabel!

2   @IBAction func pizzaType(sender : UISegmentedControl) {

3   }

4   @IBAction func sizeButton(sender : UIButton) { //blue button

5   }

6   @IBAction func clearDisplayButton(sender : UIButton) { //red button

7   }

Finish Setting up the View

In the last post in this series, we used a slider to specify pizza size. We will use preset buttons this time. We are going to use our blue sizeButton to specify the size in its label. Go back into interface builder and click once on the blue button. Copy the button, then paste it 6 times. Change the titles and arrange the buttons to look like this:

Finished Layout

In case you have never done this before, this is a way to have multiple buttons use the same IBAction. The properties can be different for the buttons, in our case the titles, but they react exactly the same to being pressed. Our model will take the title string and convert it into a pizza size.

Make the Basic Model and Properties

Between the import and the class ViewController: code, make a little space and add the following:

```
1    class Pizza
2    {
3        let pi = 3.1415926
4        let maxPizza = 24.0
5
6        var pizzaDiameter = 0.0
7        var pizzaType = "Cheese"
8    }
```

With that small amount of code, we created a class with two properties and two constants. That's it. Swift does require initialized values, thus we have to specify an initialization value. This is to allow implicit typing to figure out what type to use. When we declare a variable in a class in Swift, it becomes a property of that class. Similarly declaring a constant becomes a constant of the class.

Add a Method..or is it a Function?

Adding methods is also easy. We did it last time in the view controller. A function within a class becomes a method of that class.

A Computational Method

Add the following under var pizzaType = "Cheese"

```
1     func pizzaArea() -> Double{
2          return radius * radius * pi
3     }
```

We have not had a case yet where we return a value until now. The pizzaArea() method returns a double. In Objective-C, and many C syntax languges we have the return value first, something like -(Double)pizzaArea{} In Swift, the return value is on the end with an operator -> to specify the type of the return value. if there is no return value, it is the equivalent of (void) in C-syntax languages. In this case we return the area.

We are getting a syntax error now since radius is not defined. We'll come back to radius shortly and show one of the really cool features of Swift.

Swift's Switch Switch

Swift made a few changes to the switch control Add this method under pizzaArea():

```
1     func diameterFromString(aString:NSString) -> Double {
2          switch aString {
3          case "Personal":
4              return 8.0
5          case "10\"":
6              return 10.0
7          case "12\"":
8              return 12.0
9          case "16\"","15\"":
10             return 16.0
```

```
11        case &quot;18\&quot;&quot;:
12            return 18.0
13        case &quot;24\&quot;&quot;:
14            return 24.0
15        default:
16            return 0.0
17        }
```

Switch in Swift does not use breaks. We can also list several cases for each case, so a 15" and a 16" pizza returns 16. The Swift switch does need all cases be covered, so the default: case is mandatory to catch everything not stipulated above the default.

This method also has a parameter. We specify the variable name and then the type, separated by a colon for parameters.

Create Computed Properties

We earler found we needed the radius. We could make a method to do this, but there is another, better way. Add the following code between the pizzaArea() and the var pizzaType="Cheese" declaration.

```
1     var radius : Double {  //computed property
2         get{   //must define a getter
3             return pizzaDiameter/2.0
4         }
5         set(newRadius){ //optionally define a setter
6             pizzaDiameter = newRadius * 2.0
7         }
8     }
```

```
9

10     var area :  Double {

11       get{

12         return pizzaArea()

13       }
```

Line 1 and line 10 declares a computed property, a property based on the values of other properties. Computed properties must declare their type, and must include a getter. Within the block after the declaration, we declare a getter named get which returns a value computed by the already declared property pizzaDiameter. Optionally you can include a setter for the property, as we did in line 5 for the radius. In our second example, we made a second computed property with only a getter for the area, which uses a method in our class.

Use the Model in the Controller

We can now use our model in our code. Before we do let's write a handler for the clear button. Change clearDisplayButton to this:

```
1     @IBAction func clearDisplayButton(sender : UIButton) {

2         resultsDisplayLabel.text = clearString

3     }
```

For our initial setup change viewDidLoad to this:

```
1     override func viewDidLoad() {

2       super.viewDidLoad()

3       resultsDisplayLabel.text = clearString

4       view.backgroundColor = UIColor(red:0.99,green:0.9,blue:0.9,alpha:1.0)

5     }
```

Just under the view controller's class declaration add the following:

```
1    let pizza = Pizza()
```

```
2    let clearString = &quot;I Like Pizza!&quot;
```

Line 2 is a simple string constant declaration used for clearing the label. Line 1 is all we need to instantiate a pizza object: declare the object as a constant and give a class for the object. In Swift we say goodbye to alloc and init and even pointers. Even thoughpizza is a constant, its properties are not constants. This works, and keeps better memory allocation than using var. Now add a display method for the label:

```
1    func displayPizza(){
```

```
2      let displayString = NSString(format:&quot;%6.1f inch %@ Pizza&quot;,pizza.pizzaDiameter, pizza
```

```
3      resultsDisplayLabel.text = displayString
```

```
4    }
```

In line 2, we use dot notation to use the properties of the pizza instance. We do the same for methods as well. Add the following code for the size button:

```
1    @IBAction func sizeButton(sender : UIButton) {
```

```
2       pizza.pizzaDiameter = pizza.diameterFromString(sender.titleLabel!.text!)
```

```
3       displayPizza()
```

```
4    }
```

The size button reads the title of the button called sender, and assigns the correct size for a pizza to pizza. Line 2 calls in pizza the method diameterfromString() through dot notation.

Now add the handler for selecting a pizzaType:

```
1    @IBAction func pizzaType(sender : UISegmentedControl) {
```

```
2    let index = sender.selectedSegmentIndex
```

```
3    pizza.pizzaType = sender.titleForSegmentAtIndex(index)!
```

```
4    displayPizza()
```

```
5    }
```

Line 2 gets the index of the segment selected. Line 3 get a string with the type of pizza from the segement's label. You'll notice the ! after the function here and in line 2 of thesizeButton code.

This is a forced unwrap operator. For this lesson, just put them in – I'll explain them in the next lesson
We have gotten everything into place, and can now build and run.

The Working App

We didn't display anything for the area like we did in the first computer. Next time we will add some more functionality by using some collection types to our pizza computer to sell pizza by the square inch so we can calculate quickly how much to sell a pizza for.

The Whole Code

I should have made this two files: one for the model and one for the controller. However, since Swift lets me put them in one file, I did that to make copying and pasting a bit easier.

//

// ViewController.swift

// pizzaDemo version 2

// adds a model class to demonstrate class

//

// Created by Steven Lipton on 6/8/14.

```
//  Copyright (c) 2014 Steven Lipton. All rights reserved.

//

//


import UIKit


/* --------


Our model for MVC

keeps data  and calcualtions

about pizzas


note: for ease in copying I left this in one file

you can make a separate file and use import instead.


------------*/

class Pizza

{

    let pi = 3.1415926

    let maxPizza = 24.0


    var pizzaDiameter = 0.0

    var pizzaType = &quot;Cheese&quot;
```

```
var radius : Double {  //computed property

get{   //must define a getter

    return pizzaDiameter/2.0

}

set(newRadius){ //optionally define a setter

    pizzaDiameter = newRadius * 2.0

}

}


var area :  Double {

get{

    return pizzaArea()

}

}


func pizzaArea() -> Double{

    return radius * radius * pi

}


func diameterFromString(aString:NSString) -> Double {

    switch aString {

    case "Personal":

        return 8.0

    case "10\"":
```

```
            return 10.0

        case "12"":

            return 12.0

        case "16"":

            return 16.0,"15""

        case "18"":

            return 18.0

        case "24"":

            return 24.0

        default:

            return 0.0

        }

    }


}


/*----------



The View Controller



----------------*/



class ViewController: UIViewController {
```

```swift
let pizza = Pizza()

let clearString = "I Like Pizza!";


@IBOutlet var resultsDisplayLabel : UILabel!


func displayPizza(){

    let displayString = NSString(format:"%6.1f inch %@ Pizza",pizza.pizzaDiameter,
pizza.pizzaType)

    resultsDisplayLabel.text = displayString

}


@IBAction func pizzaType(sender : UISegmentedControl) {

    let index = sender.selectedSegmentIndex

    pizza.pizzaType = sender.titleForSegmentAtIndex(index)!

    displayPizza()

}


@IBAction func sizeButton(sender : UIButton) {

    pizza.pizzaDiameter = pizza.diameterFromString(sender.titleLabel!.text!)

    displayPizza()

}


@IBAction func clearDisplayButton(sender : UIButton) {

    resultsDisplayLabel.text = clearString
```

```
    }


    override func viewDidLoad() {

        super.viewDidLoad()

        resultsDisplayLabel.text = clearString

        view.backgroundColor = UIColor(red:0.99,green:0.9,blue:0.9,alpha:1.0)

    }


    override func didReceiveMemoryWarning() {

        super.didReceiveMemoryWarning()

        // Dispose of any resources that can be recreated.

    }


}
```

3.3 Creating Basic Interaction

Interoperability is the ability to interface between Swift and Objective-C in either direction, letting you access and use pieces of code written in one language in a file of the other language. As you begin to integrate Swift into your app development workflow, it's a good idea to understand how you can leverage interoperability to redefine, improve, and enhance the way you write Cocoa apps.

One important aspect of interoperability is that it lets you work with Objective-C APIs when writing Swift code. After you import an Objective-C framework, you can instantiate classes from it and interact with them using native Swift syntax.

Initialization

To instantiate an Objective-C class in Swift, you call one of its initializers with Swift syntax. When Objective-Cinit methods come over to Swift, they take on native Swift initializer syntax. The "init" prefix gets sliced off and becomes a keyword to indicate that the method is an initializer. For init methods that begin with "initWith," the "With" also gets sliced off. The first letter of the selector piece that had "init" or "initWith" split off from it becomes lowercase, and that selector piece is treated as the name of the first argument. The rest of the selector pieces also correspond to argument names. Each selector piece goes inside the parentheses and is required at the call site.

For example, where in Objective-C you would do this:

UITableView *myTableView = [[UITableView alloc] initWithFrame:CGRectZero style:UITableViewStyleGrouped];

In Swift, you do this:

let myTableView: UITableView = UITableView(frame: CGRectZero, style: .Grouped)

You don't need to call alloc; Swift correctly handles this for you. Notice that "init" doesn't appear anywhere when calling the Swift-style initializer.

You can be explicit in typing the object during initialization, or you can omit the type. Swift's type inference correctly determines the type of the object.

let myTextField = UITextField(frame: CGRect(x: 0.0, y: 0.0, width: 200.0, height: 40.0))

These UITableView and UITextField objects have the same familiar functionality that they have in Objective-C. You can use them in the same way you would in Objective-C, accessing any properties and calling any methods defined on the respective classes.

For consistency and simplicity, Objective-C factory methods get mapped as convenience initializers in Swift. This mapping allows them to be used with the same concise, clear syntax as initializers. For example, whereas in Objective-C you would call this factory method like this:

UIColor *color = [UIColor colorWithRed:0.5 green:0.0 blue:0.5 alpha:1.0];

In Swift, you call it like this:

let color = UIColor(red: 0.5, green: 0.0, blue: 0.5, alpha: 1.0)

Failable Initialization

In Objective-C, initializers directly return the object they initialize. To inform the caller when initialization has failed, an Objective-C initializer can return nil. In Swift, this pattern is built into a language feature calledfailable initialization.

Many Objective-C initializers in iOS and OS X system frameworks have been audited to indicate whether initialization can fail. You can indicate whether initializers in your own Objective-C classes can fail usingnullability annotations, as described in Nullability and Optionals. Objective-C initializers that indicate whether they're failable are imported as either init(...)—if initialization cannot fail—or init?(...)—if initialization can fail. Otherwise, Objective-C initializers are imported as init!(...).

For example, the UIImage(contentsOfFile:) initializer can fail to initialize a UIImage object if an image file doesn't exist at the provided path. You can use optional binding to unwrap the result of a failable initializer if initialization is successful.

if let image = UIImage(contentsOfFile: "MyImage.png") {

// loaded the image successfully

} else {

// could not load the image

}

Accessing Properties

Objective-C property declarations using the @property syntax are imported as Swift properties in the following way:

- Properties with the nullability property attributes (nonnull, nullable, and null_resettable) are imported as Swift properties with optional or non-optional type as described in Nullability and Optionals.

- Properties with the readonly property attribute are imported as Swift computed properties with a getter ({ get }).

- Properties with the weak property attribute are imported as Swift properties marked with the weakkeyword (weak var).

- Properties with an ownership property attribute other than weak (that is, assign, copy, strong, orunsafe_unretained) are imported as Swift properties with the appropriate storage.

- Atomicity property attributes (atomic and nonatomic) are ignored by Swift. All Swift properties arenonatomic.

- Accessor property attributes (getter= and setter=) are ignored by Swift.

You access properties on Objective-C objects in Swift using dot syntax, using the name of the property without parentheses.

For example, you can set the textColor and text properties of a UITextField with the following code:

myTextField.textColor = UIColor.darkGrayColor()

myTextField.text = "Hello world"

NOTE

darkGrayColor() is followed by parentheses, because darkGrayColor() is a class method on UIColor, not a property.

Objective-C methods that return a value and take no arguments can be called like an Objective-C property using dot syntax. However, these are imported by Swift as instance methods, as only Objective-C @propertydeclarations are imported by Swift as properties. Methods are imported and called as described in Working with Methods.

Working with Methods

When calling Objective-C methods from Swift, use dot syntax.

When Objective-C methods come over to Swift, the first part of an Objective-C selector becomes the base method name and appears outside the parentheses. The first argument appears immediately inside the parentheses, without a name. The rest of the selector pieces correspond to argument names and go inside the parentheses. All selector pieces are required at the call site.

For example, whereas in Objective-C you would do this:

[myTableView insertSubview:mySubview atIndex:2];

In Swift, you do this:

myTableView.insertSubview(mySubview, atIndex: 2)

If you're calling a method with no arguments, you must still include the parentheses.

myTableView.layoutIfNeeded()

id Compatibility

Swift includes a protocol type named AnyObject that represents any kind of object, just as id does in Objective-C. The AnyObject protocol allows you to write type-safe Swift code while maintaining the flexibility of an untyped object. Because of the additional safety provided by the AnyObject protocol, Swift imports id asAnyObject.

For example, as with id, you can assign an object of any class type to a constant or variable typed asAnyObject. You can also reassign a variable to an object of a different type.

var myObject: AnyObject = UITableViewCell()

myObject = NSDate()

You can also call any Objective-C method and access any property without casting to a more specific class type. This includes Objective-C compatible methods marked with the @objc attribute.

let futureDate = myObject.dateByAddingTimeInterval(10)

let timeSinceNow = myObject.timeIntervalSinceNow

However, because the specific type of an object typed as AnyObject is not known until runtime, it is possible to inadvertently write unsafe code. As in Objective-C, if you invoke a method or access a property that does not exist on an AnyObject typed object, it is a runtime error. For example, the following code compiles without complaint and then causes an unrecognized selector error at runtime:

myObject.characterAtIndex(5)

// crash, myObject doesn't respond to that method

You can take advantage of optionals in Swift to eliminate this common Objective-C error from your code. When you call an Objective-C method on an AnyObject type object, the method call actually behaves like an implicitly unwrapped optional. You can use the same optional chaining syntax you would use for optional methods in protocols to optionally invoke a method on AnyObject.

NOTE

Property access on AnyObject always returns an optional value.

For example, in the code listing below, the first and second lines are not executed because the countproperty and the characterAtIndex: method do not exist on an NSDate object. The myCount constant is inferred to be an optional Int, and is set to nil. You can also use an if–let statement to conditionally unwrap the result of a method that the object may not respond to, as shown on line three.

```
let myCount = myObject.count

let myChar = myObject.characterAtIndex?(5)

if let fifthCharacter = myObject.characterAtIndex?(5) {

print("Found \(fifthCharacter) at index 5")

}
```

As with all downcasts in Swift, casting from AnyObject to a more specific object type is not guaranteed to succeed and therefore returns an optional value. You can check that optional value to determine whether the cast succeeded.

```
let userDefaults = NSUserDefaults.standardUserDefaults()

let lastRefreshDate: AnyObject? = userDefaults.objectForKey("LastRefreshDate")

if let date = lastRefreshDate as? NSDate {

print("\(date.timeIntervalSinceReferenceDate)")

}
```

Ofcourse, if you are certain of the type of the object (and know that it is not nil), you can force the invocation with the as operator.

```
let myDate = lastRefreshDate as! NSDate
```

let timeInterval = myDate.timeIntervalSinceReferenceDate

Nullability and Optionals

In Objective-C, you work with references to objects using raw pointers that could be NULL (referred to as nilin Objective-C). In Swift, all values—including structures and object references—are guaranteed to be non–null. Instead, you represent a value that could be missing by wrapping the type of the value in an optional type. When you need to indicate that a value is missing, you use the value nil. For more information about optionals, see Optionals in The Swift Programming Language.

Objective-C can use nullability annotations to designate whether a parameter type, property type, or return type, can have a NULL or nil value. Individual type declarations can be audited using the _Nullable and_Nonnull annotations, individual property declarations can be audited using the nullable, nonnull andnull_resettable property attributes, or entire regions can be audited for nullability using theNS_ASSUME_NONNULL_BEGIN and NS_ASSUME_NONNULL_END macros. If no nullability information is provided for a type, Swift cannot distinguish between optional and non-optional references, and imports it as an implicitly unwrapped optional.

Types declared to be nullable, either with a _Nonnull annotation or in an audited region, are imported by Swift as a non-optional.

Types declared to be nullable with a _Nullable annotation, are imported by Swift as an optional.

Types declared without a nullability annotation are imported by Swift as an implicitly unwrapped optional.

For example, consider the following Objective-C declarations:

@property (nullable) id nullableProperty;

@property (nonnull) id nonNullProperty;

@property id unannotatedProperty;

NS_ASSUME_NONNULL_BEGIN

- (id)returnsNonNullValue;

```
- (void)takesNonNullParameter:(id)value;

NS_ASSUME_NONNULL_END


- (nullable id)returnsNullableValue;

- (void)takesNullableParameter:(nullable id)value;


- (id)returnsUnannotatedValue;

- (void)takesUnannotatedParameter:(id)value;
```

Here's how they're imported by Swift:

```
var nullableProperty: AnyObject?

var nonNullProperty: AnyObject

var unannotatedProperty: AnyObject!


func returnsNonNullValue() -> AnyObject

func takesNonNullParameter(value: AnyObject)


func returnsNullableValue() -> AnyObject?

func takesNullableParameter(value: AnyObject?)


func returnsUnannotatedValue() -> AnyObject!

func takesUnannotatedParameter(value: AnyObject!)
```

Most of the Objective-C system frameworks, including Foundation, already provide nullability annotations, allowing you to work with values in an idiomatic and type-safe manner.

Extensions

A Swift extension is similar to an Objective-C category. Extensions expand the behavior of existing classes, structures, and enumerations, including those defined in Objective-C. You can define an extension on a type from either a system framework or one of your own custom types. Simply import the appropriate module, and refer to the class, structure, or enumeration by the same name that you would use in Objective-C.

For example, you can extend the UIBezierPath class to create a simple Bézier path with an equilateral triangle, based on a provided side length and starting point.

```
extension UIBezierPath {

convenience init(triangleSideLength: CGFloat, origin: CGPoint) {

self.init()

let squareRoot = CGFloat(sqrt(3.0))

let altitude = (squareRoot * triangleSideLength) / 2

moveToPoint(origin)

addLineToPoint(CGPoint(x: origin.x + triangleSideLength, y: origin.y))

addLineToPoint(CGPoint(x: origin.x + triangleSideLength / 2, y: origin.y + altitude))

closePath()

}

}
```

You can use extensions to add properties (including class and static properties). However, these properties must be computed; extensions can't add stored properties to classes, structures, or enumerations.

This example extends the CGRect structure to contain a computed area property:

```
extension CGRect {

var area: CGFloat {

return width * height
```

```
}

}
```

let rect = CGRect(x: 0.0, y: 0.0, width: 10.0, height: 50.0)

let area = rect.area

You can also use extensions to add protocol conformance to a class without subclassing it. If the protocol is defined in Swift, you can also add conformance to it to structures or enumerations, whether defined in Swift or Objective-C.

You cannot use extensions to override existing methods or properties on Objective-C types.

Closures

Objective-C blocks are automatically imported as Swift closures with Objective-C block calling convention, denoted by the @convention(block) attribute. For example, here is an Objective-C block variable:

```
void (^completionBlock)(NSData *, NSError *) = ^(NSData *data, NSError *error) {

// ...

}
```

And here's what it looks like in Swift:

```
let completionBlock: (NSData, NSError) -> Void = { (data, error) in

// ...

}
```

Swift closures and Objective-C blocks are compatible, so you can pass Swift closures to Objective-C methods that expect blocks. Swift closures and functions have the same type, so you can even pass the name of a Swift function.

Closures have similar capture semantics as blocks but differ in one key way: Variables are mutable rather than copied. In other words, the behavior of __block in Objective-C is the default behavior for variables in Swift.

Object Comparison

There are two distinct types of comparison when you compare two objects in Swift. The first, equality (==), compares the contents of the objects. The second, identity (===), determines whether or not the constants or variables refer to the same object instance.

Swift and Objective-C objects are typically compared in Swift using the == and === operators. Swift provides a default implementation of the == operator for objects that derive from the NSObject class. In the implementation of this operator, Swift invokes the isEqual: method defined on the NSObject class. TheNSObject class only performs an identity comparison, so you should implement your own isEqual: method in classes that derive from the NSObject class. Because you can pass Swift objects (including ones not derived from NSObject) to Objective-C APIs, you should implement the isEqual: method for these classes if you want the Objective-C APIs to compare the contents of the objects rather than their identities.

As part of implementing equality for your class, be sure to implement the hash property according to the rules in Object comparison. Further, if you want to use your class as keys in a dictionary, also conform to the Hashable protocol and implement the hashValue property.

Swift Type Compatibility

When you create a Swift class that descends from an Objective-C class, the class and its members—properties, methods, subscripts, and initializers—are automatically available from Objective-C. In some cases, you need finer grained control over how your Swift API is exposed to Objective-C. You can use the@objc attribute if your Swift class doesn't inherit from an Objective-C class, or if you want to change the name of a symbol in your interface as it's exposed to Objective-C code. You can also use the dynamicmodifier to require that access to members be dynamically dispatched through the Objective-C runtime if you're using APIs like key–value observing that dynamically replace the implementation of a method.

Exposing Swift Interfaces in Objective-C

When you define a Swift class that inherits from NSObject or any other Objective-C class, the class is automatically compatible with Objective-C. All of the steps in this section have already been done for you by the Swift compiler. If you never import a Swift class in Objective-C code, you don't need to worry about type compatibility in this case as well. Otherwise, if your Swift class does not derive from an Objective-C class and you want to use it from Objective-C code, you can use the @objc attribute described below.

The @objc attribute makes your Swift API available in Objective-C and the Objective-C runtime. In other words, you can use the @objc attribute before a Swift method, property, subscript, initializer, class, or enumeration to use it from Objective-C code.

NOTE

Nested type declarations cannot be annotated with the @objc attribute.

Only Swift enumerations that declare a basic integer type, such as Int, as its raw value type can use the@objc attribute.

If your class inherits from an Objective-C class, the compiler inserts the attribute for you. The compiler also adds the attribute to every member in a class that is itself marked with the @objc attribute. When you use the@IBOutlet, @IBAction, or @NSManaged attribute, the @objc attribute is added as well. This attribute is also useful when you're working with Objective-C classes that use selectors to implement the target-action design pattern—for example, NSTimer or UIButton.

NOTE

The compiler does not automatically insert the @objc attribute for declarations marked with the privateaccess-level modifier.

When you use a Swift API from Objective-C, the compiler typically performs a direct translation. For example, the Swift API func playSong(name: String) is imported as - (void)playSong:(NSString *)name in Objective-C. However, there is one exception: When you use a Swift initializer in Objective-C, the compiler adds the text "initWith" to the beginning of the method and properly capitalizes the first character in the original initializer. For example, this Swift initializer init (songName: String, artist: String) is imported as - (instancetype)initWithSongName:(NSString *)songName artist:(NSString *)artist in Objective-C.

Swift also provides a variant of the @objc attribute that allows you to specify name for your symbol in Objective-C. For example, if the name of your Swift class contains a character that isn't supported by Objective-C, you can provide an alternative name to use in Objective-C. If you provide an Objective-C name for a Swift function, use Objective-C selector syntax. Remember to add a colon (:) wherever a parameter follows a selector piece.

@objc(Squirrel)

class Белка: NSObject {

```
@objc(initWithName:)

init (имя: String) {

// ...

}

@objc(hideNuts:inTree:)

func прячьОрехи(количество: Int, вДереве дерево: Дерево) {

// ...

}

}
```

When you use the @objc(name) attribute on a Swift class, the class is made available in Objective-C without any namespacing. As a result, this attribute can also be useful when you migrate an archivable Objective-C class to Swift. Because archived objects store the name of their class in the archive, you should use the@objc(name) attribute to specify the same name as your Objective-C class so that older archives can be unarchived by your new Swift class.

NOTE

Conversely, Swift also provides the @nonobjc attribute, which makes a Swift declaration unavailable in Objective-C. You can use it to resolve circularity for bridging methods and to allow overloading of methods for classes marked @objc. If an Objective-C method is overridden by a Swift method that cannot be represented in Objective-C, such as by specifying a parameter to be a variable, that method must be marked @nonobjc.

Requiring Dynamic Dispatch

While the @objc attribute exposes your Swift API to the Objective-C runtime, it does not guarantee dynamic dispatch of a property, method, subscript, or initializer. The Swift compiler may still devirtualize or inline member access to optimize the performance of your code, bypassing the Objective-C runtime. When you mark a member declaration with the dynamic modifier, access to that member is always dynamically dispatched. Because declarations marked with the dynamic modifier are dispatched using the Objective-C runtime, they're implicitly marked with the @objc attribute.

Requiring dynamic dispatch is rarely necessary. However, you must use the dynamic modifier when you know that the implementation of an API is replaced at runtime. For example, you can use themethod_exchangeImplementations function in the Objective-C runtime to swap out the implementation of a method while an app is running. If the Swift compiler inlined the implementation of the method or devirtualized access to it, the new implementation would not be used.

Lightweight Generics

Objective-C declarations of NSArray, NSSet and NSDictionary types using lightweight generic parameterization are imported by Swift with information about the type of their contents preserved.

For example, consider the following Objective-C property declarations:

@property NSArray<NSDate *> *dates;

@property NSSet<NSString *> *words;

@property NSDictionary<NSURL *, NSData *> *cachedData;

Here's how Swift imports them:

var dates: [NSDate]

var words: Set<String>

var cachedData: [NSURL: NSData]

NOTE:

Aside from these Foundation collection classes, Objective-C lightweight generics are ignored by Swift. Any other types using lightweight generics are imported into Swift as if they were unparameterized.

Objective-C Selectors

An Objective-C selector is a type that refers to the name of an Objective-C method. In Swift, Objective-C selectors are represented by the Selector structure. You can construct a selector with a string literal, such as let mySelector: Selector = "tappedButton:". Because string literals can be automatically converted to selectors, you can pass a string literal to any method that accepts a selector.

```
import UIKit

class MyViewController: UIViewController {

let myButton = UIButton(frame: CGRect(x: 0, y: 0, width: 100, height: 50))


override init?(nibName nibNameOrNil: String?, bundle nibBundleOrNil: NSBundle?) {

super.init(nibName: nibNameOrNil, bundle: nibBundleOrNil)

myButton.addTarget(self, action: "tappedButton:", forControlEvents: .TouchUpInside)

}


func tappedButton(sender: UIButton!) {

print("tapped button")

}


required init?(coder: NSCoder) {

super.init(coder: coder)

}

}
```

NOTE

The performSelector: method and related selector-invoking methods are not imported in Swift because they are inherently unsafe.

If your Swift class inherits from an Objective-C class, all of the methods and properties in the class are available as Objective-C selectors. Otherwise, if your Swift class does not inherit from an Objective-C class, you need to prefix the symbol you want to use as a selector with the @objc attribute, as described in Swift Type Compatibility.

3.4 Creating Quick Connections

Create an action connection to send a message from a control to your code. When the user clicks a button control, for example, the button should send an action message telling your code to execute an appropriate action.

1. In the project navigator, select a storyboard or xib file.

The file's contents open in Interface Builder.

2. In Interface Builder, select the control you want to configure by clicking it in the outline view or on the canvas.

A control is a user interface object—such as a button, text field, switch, scroll bar, or slider—that causes instant actions or visible results when the user manipulates the object. If the outline view doesn't appear, display it by clicking the Show Document Outline (▭) control in the lower-left corner of the canvas. Select a control from the list of nested objects.

3. Choose View > Assistant Editor > Show Assistant Editor.

The assistant editor opens your object's implementation file.

4. Control-drag from the control in Interface Builder to the implementation file.

Xcode indicates where you can insert an action method in your code. (In the screenshot, the assistant editor displays the implementation file of the view controller for the Warrior button.)

The connections panel and the Connections inspector allow you to create multiple connections for the same object in quick succession. Control-click a control and release the mouse button to display a connections panel, or choose View > Utilities > Show Connections Inspector to display the Connections inspector. Click in the circle to the right of an action, and drag over the target object for the connection. (If the target is not visible, hover over it to open and reveal the children.)

If an object does not highlight, it's not of the right type and cannot be connected to the source object. If the target object highlights, release the mouse button. Interface Builder displays a list of the target object's action methods. Select the desired action method to finish the connection.

3.5 Understanding The Cocoa Application Life Cycle

A lot of developers really want to know what's actually happening inside of a Cocoa Application, inside of a Cocoa project, even a basic one that we have just created here. What do these other files represent? What really is this AppDelegate? And why, if this is an Objective-C program, don't we do anything with the main function to begin an App? And if we are using this MainMenu.xib, where is the code that actually loads that? Well, let's take a look at the processes here.

There is a predefined C function in Cocoa that creates a new object called NSApplication. So the basic process is main opens up, calls the NSApplicationMain function that creates this NSApplication object that represents the standard Cocoa Application, the foundation, the plumbing, the core functionality that every Cocoa Application is going to need, setting up a run loop, so the application stays active, responding to events and so on.

In a lot of other languages, on other platforms, you would use inheritance for this. You'd actually inherit from this NSApplication object, or in other languages, an application class. Well, in Cocoa, we don't use inheritance for this. We use delegation. We need to have an Objective-C class in our project that will act as the delegate for the standard built-in NSApplication object.

So the NSApplication object can let our delegate class know about various events we might be interested in, and we can choose whether or not a respond to them. Now at the same time, the NSApplicationMain function knows we want at least an initial user interface, so it's going to look in a property list file in our Xcode project that contains the name of our main xib file. And by default, that is MainMenu.xib. And that xib file--and everything in it--Menus, the Window, the other user interface elements, will be loaded as part of the startup process and exist for the life time of the application.

Now in Cocoa, we can provide multiple windows--but we will see that a little later--and by default, that app delegate will be connected to our main window object. And all of this is provided for us as a basic framework. So in main.m, we call NSApplicationMain. If I look at this Lifecycle-info.plist, it's whatever your project is called -info.plist, we will find an entry in here called the Main nib file base name, which here it says MainMenu, that's what's loading in MainMenu.xib and everything inside it.

And when looking at the project files, you might also have a pretty good guess of what class is acting as the delegate for the application object, it is Ofcourse here the AppDelegate object.So this is where we could put the code to respond to application level events like, for example, our applicationFinishingLaunching and later maybe the applicationTerminating. Now as we have seen, we can also put code in this class to react to events in our interface, the same class can act as an application delegate, and there is a controller for our view objects, although and anything nontrivial, will split that out into another class. And if you finding this all a little intimidating, fair enough, there is a lot going on here, but here's the thing.

You don't touch main, you don't touch NSApplicationMain. Most of the times you don't need to touch this plist entry. This is the framework that is provided for you. Your interaction with this provided structure is first off to add code into the app delegate to deal with application level events, laying out your user interface in the xib file and then creating Objective-C classes to behave as models and controllers and hooking them altogether.

So when the application first launches, you will automatically hav

3.6 Diagnosing Connection Issues

Once you get past things like simple typos, missing semicolons, and case-sensitivity problems in Objective-C. The single-most common stumbling block for new developers in Cocoa is making a mistake with the connections, dragging from the wrong object in your user interface to the wrong part of your code. And the symptom of these problems is annoying because it's often nothing. Incorrect connections rarely cause a bug or a message, instead nothing happens when you expect something should happen.

You click a button, and you expect it to call a method to change a label, and it doesn't. Well, here perhaps the button isn't hooked up to the method. Perhaps the Text field isn't hooked up to the code, perhaps the method isn't doing what it should, or perhaps they are both fine, but the label isn't hooked up. So if we have no actual error from Xcode we first go looking at our connections. And typically you drive this from the XIB file. So I'm going to quit out of this application and jump into this MainMenu.xib.

Now there is no one master view of all the existing connections in your user interface, you go object-by-object, element-by-element, looking at the connections for each object. So know that you can view these connections in several different ways. You can right-click on each element-- or Ctrl and single-click does the same thing.

Every Sent Action needs two pieces of information, the target and the action. The target is the class this button should point to, and right now it's pointing to the App Delegate class, although it could be any class.

3.7 Creating Custom Controller Classes

Every Objective-C class, except NSObject, is based on (and inherits from) another class. The NSObject class itself is the most fundamental Objective-C class, because it defines the basic behavior of all objects and is at the root of all inheritance hierarchies. Because we don't need any special behavior in our Calculator other than what is already defined in the AppKit, our Controller class will be a subclass of NSObject. We'll start building our Controller class by subclassing it from the NSObject class in IB.

1. Click the Classes tab in IB's Nib File window to view the AppKit's object hierarchy.

2. Scroll to the far left in the Classes pane using the horizontal scroller at the bottom of the Nib File window, and then select the NSObject class by clicking it. You can also rapidly jump to the NSObject class by typing the word "NSObject" into the Classes pane's Search field.

3. The NSObject class name is displayed in gray, which means that you can't change any of its properties or built-in behaviors without subclassing it. So that's what we'll have to do. 3. Click IB's Classes menu item at the top of the screen, then choose Subclass NSObject, as shown in Figure (or simply hit the Return key when NSObject is highlighted).

Figure 5-11. Classes menu in IB

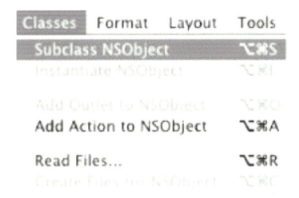

4. A new class called MyObject will appear under NSObject in the class hierarchy.

5. Change the name from "MyObject" to "Controller", and hit Return. You've just created a new Objective-C class called Controller. Right now it doesn't do anything different from the NSObject class. Next, we'll give the Controller class some custom behavior by adding some outlets and actions.

3.8 Creating Alert Panels and Alert Sheets

Sheets implement window modal (as opposed to application modal) dialogs that are attached to the window. Thus, when a dialog pops up asking for attention, it blocks interaction only with that particular window, not the entire application. When a sheet is opened or closed, it appears to slide out of the title bar. Because the sheet is attached to another window, such as a document window, the user never loses track of what dialog belongs with which window. Figure 3-8 shows an example of a sheet.

Figure - A TextEdit sheet asking if you want to save changes

The Application Kit defines a number of convenient functions for displaying standard alert and message sheets, including NSBeginAlertSheet,NSBegin-InformationalAlertSheet,

and NSBeginCriticalAlertSheet. Each function takes the same parameters; they differ only in the icon displayed on the left of the sheet. The function prototype for NSBeginAlertSheet is the following:

void NSBeginAlertSheet(NSString *title,

NSString *defaultButton,

NSString *alternateButton,

NSString *otherButton,

NSWindow *docWindow,

id modalDelegate,

SEL didEndSelector,

SEL didDismissSelector,

void *contextInfo,

NSString *msg, ...)

Parameter	Description
Title	The title of the sheet, displayed at the top of the sheet in bold-faced font.
defaultButton	The title of the sheet's default button, generally "OK". Passing nil or an empty string will give a localized default button title (i.e., "OK" in English).
alternateButton	The title of the sheet's alternate button, such as "Don't Save," that appears on the left side of the sheet when three buttons are present. Passing nil causes this button to not be created.
otherButton	Title for a third button, such as "Cancel", that appears in the middle. Passing nil causes this button to not be created.
docWindow	The window to which the sheet is attached.
modalDelegate	The object that handles user interaction with the sheet.
didEndSelector	A selector of the method implemented by the modal delegate that will be invoked when the modal session is ended, but before the sheet is dismissed.
didDismissSelector	Selector of the method implemented by the modal delegate is invoked after the sheet is dismissed. This may be NULL if you don't want to end a didDismissSelector.
contextInfo	Pointer to additional data to be passed to didEndSelector or didDismissSelector.
msg	A printf formatted message to be displayed in the sheet. Optional printf-style arguments may follow the message.

An alert similar to the one in Figure can be created with a call to NSBeginInformationalAlertSheet, as shown in Example 3-2.

Example 3-2. Creating an alert sheet with NSBeginInformationalAlertSheet

NSBeginInformationalAlertSheet(

@"Do you want to save changes to \

```
        this document before closing?"

    @"Save",

    @"Don't Save",

    @"Cancel",

    mainWindow,

    self,

    @selector(sheetDidEnd:returnCode:contextInfo:),

    NULL,

    NULL,

    @"If you don't save, your changes will be lost.");
```

You can display any window as a sheet by using APIs provided by NSApplication. To display a sheet, invoke the following method:

beginSheet:modalForWindow:

  modalDelegate:didEndSelector:contextInfo:

The first argument, beginSheet:, is the NSWindow we wish to display as a sheet. The modalForWindow: argument specifies the window to which the sheet is attached. Since application execution continues while a sheet is open, the sheet uses a modal delegate to handle user interaction. This delegate is assigned in the modalDelegate: argument. The callback method is indicated in didEndSelector: and has the following signature:

- (void)sheetDidEnd:(NSWindow *)sheet

    returnCode:(int)returnCode

    contextInfo:(void *)contextInfo;

In this method, contextInfo: is the object passed in the NSApplication method used to open the sheet. It is used to optionally pass arbitrary information between the creator of the sheet and the modal delegate.

To end a document modal session, use NSApplication's methods endSheet: or endSheet:returnCode:. Each method takes the sheet window as a parameter. The second, endSheet:returnCode:, also takes an integer return code that is passed to the didEndSelector: method. Example 3-3 shows how to open and close a sheet in an application.

Example 3-3. Using sheets in an application

```
/*

 * This method is invoked to open a sheet.

 * Assume sheetWindow and mainWindow are Interface Builder

 * outlet instance variables connected to windows in a nib.

 */

- (void)openSheet:(id)sender

{

   SEL selector = @selector(sheetDidEnd:returnCode:contextInfo:);


   [NSApp beginSheet:sheetWindow

     modalForWindow:mainWindow

      modalDelegate:self

     didEndSelector:selector

       contextInfo:NULL];

}


/*

 * This could be the action of the "Cancel" button of the sheet

 * in Figure 3-8.

 */

- (void)cancelSheet:(id)sender
```

```
{

    [NSApp endSheet:sheetWindow returnCode:NSCancelButton];

}


/*

 * This could be the action of the "Save" button of the sheet

 * in Figure 3-8.

 */

- (void)acceptSheet:(id)sender

{

    [NSApp endSheet:sheetWindow returnCode:NSOKButton];

}


- (void)sheetDidEnd:(NSWindow *)sheet

    returnCode:(int)returnCode

    contextInfo:(void *)contextInfo

{

  /*

    * Can do something here based on the value of returnCode

    * or do something in the button actions themselves.

    */

  if ( returnCode == NSOKButton ) {

      // If OK was clicked...

  } else if ( returnCode == NSCancelButton ) {
```

```
    // If Cancel was clicked....

}
```

```
  [sheet orderOut:nil];

}
```

In this example, NSOKButton and NSCancelButton are global constants often used to identify those buttons in a dialog. The endSheet: methods only end the document modal session; they do not remove the sheet from the screen. To hide the sheet, send an orderOut: message to the sheet window.

Finally, there are yet more ways to display sheets: the AppKit classes that implement standard Mac OS X user interfaces, such as NSPrintPanel andNSOpenPanel, all provide ways to display their respective interfaces as document modal sheets.

Chapter 4: Delegation

It is a technique for specifying objects that perform functions for other objects.

A delegate is an object that acts on behalf of, or in coordination with, another object when that object encounters an event in a program. The delegating object is often a responder object—that is, an object inheriting from NSResponder in AppKit or UIResponder in UIKit—that is responding to a user event. The delegate is an object that is delegated control of the user interface for that event, or is at least asked to interpret the event in an application-specific manner.

To better appreciate the value of delegation, it helps to consider an off-the-shelf Cocoa object such as a text field (an instance of NSTextField or UITextField) or a table view (an instance of NSTableView or UITableView). These objects are designed to fulfill a specific role in a generic fashion; a window object in the AppKit framework, for example, responds to mouse manipulations of its controls and handles such things as closing, resizing, and moving the physical window. This restricted and generic behavior necessarily limits what the object can know about how an event affects (or will affect) something elsewhere in the application, especially when the affected behavior is specific to your application. Delegation provides a way for your custom object to communicate application-specific behavior to the off-the-shelf object.

The programming mechanism of delegation gives objects a chance to coordinate their appearance and state with changes occurring elsewhere in a program, changes usually brought about by user actions. More importantly, delegation makes it possible for one object to alter the behavior of another object without the need to inherit from it. The delegate is almost always one of your custom objects, and by definition it incorporates application-specific logic that the generic and delegating object cannot possibly know itself.

4. 1 Understanding Delegation

Delegates are especially useful when you want one object to coordinate several others. For instance, you might create an NSWindowController subclass and make it it's window's delegate. That same window might contain several other elements (like NSTextFields) that you want to make the window controller a delegate of. This way you don't need to subclass the window and several of its controls. You can keep all the code that conceptually belongs together in the same class. In addition, delegates usually belong to the controller level of the Model-View-Controller concept. By subclassing NSWindowyou would move controller type code to the view level.

A class can adopt any number of protocols, so <NSWindowDelegate, NSTextFieldDelegate> is perfectly valid. You can then set your object as the delegate of any number of windows and text fields. To find out what delegate messages a class like NSTextField supports check out the class reference.The -delegate and -setDelegate: methods will usually point you to the proper protocol. In our case this is NSTextFieldDelegate. For classes that have been added to older version of Apple's frameworks there often an additional section on delegate methods (either alongside "Class Methods" and "Instance Methods" or as a subsection of "Tasks"). Note that declaring your class as conforming to a delegate protocol will not have them magically delivered to your object – you must explicitly set it as the delegate:

```
@interface MyWindowController : NSWindowController <NSWindowDelegate, NSTextFieldDelegate> {

    NSTextField *_someTextField;

}

@property (nonatomic, retain) IBOutlet NSTextField *someTextField;


@end

@implementation MyWindowController

@synthesize someTextField = _someTextField;


- (void)dealloc {

    [_someTextField release];

    [super dealloc];

}


- (void)windowDidLoad {

    [super windowDidLoad];

    // When using a XIB/NIB, you can also set the File's Owner as the
```

```
  // delegate of the window and the text field.

  [[self window] setDelegate:self];

  [[self someTextField] setDelegate:self];

}

- (void)windowDidMiniaturize:(NSNotification *)notification {


}

- (BOOL)control:(NSControl *)control textShouldEndEditing:(NSText *)fieldEditor {

  return YES;

}

@end
```

4.2 Using The Application Delegation

The design of the delegation mechanism is simple—see Figure 3-1. The delegating class has an outlet or property, usually one that is named delegate; if it is an outlet, it includes methods for setting and accessing the value of the outlet. It also declares, without implementing, one or more methods that constitute a formal protocol or an informal protocol. A formal protocol that uses optional methods—a feature of Objective-C 2.0—is the preferred approach, but both kinds of protocols are used by the Cocoa frameworks for delegation.

In the informal protocol approach, the delegating class declares methods on a category of NSObject, and the delegate implements only those methods in which it has an interest in coordinating itself with the delegating object or affecting that object's default behavior. If the delegating class declares a formal protocol, the delegate may choose to implement those methods marked optional, but it must implement the required ones.

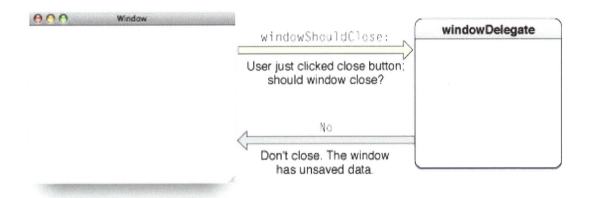

The methods of the protocol mark significant events handled or anticipated by the delegating object. This object wants either to communicate these events to the delegate or, for impending events, to request input or approval from the delegate. For example, when a user clicks the close button of a window in OS X, the window object sends the windowShouldClose: message to its delegate; this gives the delegate the opportunity to veto or defer the closing of the window if, for example, the window has associated data that must be saved.

Figure 3–2 A more realistic sequence involving a delegate

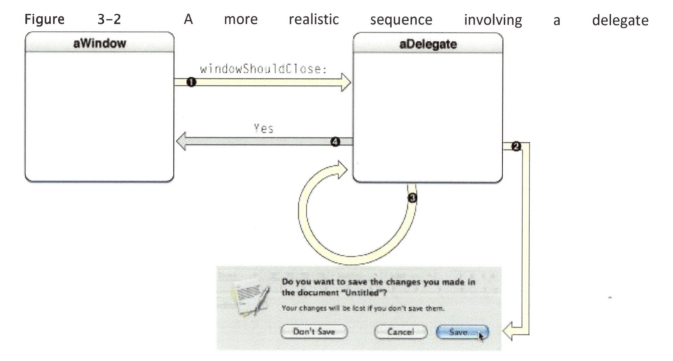

The delegating object sends a message only if the delegate implements the method. It makes this discovery by invoking the NSObjectmethod respondsToSelector:in the delegate first.

4.3 Delegation for UI elements

The Form of Delegation Messages

Delegation methods have a conventional form. They begin with the name of the AppKit or UIKit object doing the delegating—application, window, control, and so on; this name is in lower-case and without the "NS" or "UI" prefix. Usually (but not always) this object name is followed by an auxiliary verb indicative of the temporal status of the reported event. This verb, in other words, indicates whether the event is about to occur ("Should" or "Will") or whether it has just occurred ("Did" or "Has"). This temporal distinction helps to categorize those messages that expect a return value and those that don't. Listing 3-1 includes a few AppKit delegation methods that expect a return value.

```
- (BOOL)application:(NSApplication *)sender

    openFile:(NSString *)filename;                    // NSApplication

- (BOOL)application:(UIApplication *)application

    handleOpenURL:(NSURL *)url;                    // UIApplicationDelegate

- (UITableRowIndexSet *)tableView:(NSTableView *)tableView

    willSelectRows:(UITableRowIndexSet *)selection;      // UITableViewDelegate

- (NSRect)windowWillUseStandardFrame:(NSWindow *)window

    defaultFrame:(NSRect)newFrame;                    // NSWindow
```

The delegate that implements these methods can block the impending event (by returning NO in the first two methods) or alter a suggested value (the index set and the frame rectangle in the last two methods). It can even defer an impending event; for example, the delegate implementing the applicationShouldTerminate:method can delay application termination by returning NSTerminateLater.

Other delegation methods are invoked by messages that don't expect a return value and so are typed to return void. These messages are purely informational, and the method names often contain "Did", "Will", or some other indication of a transpired or impending event. Listing 3-2 shows a few examples of these kinds of delegation method.

```
- (void) tableView:(NSTableView*)tableView

    mouseDownInHeaderOfTableColumn:(NSTableColumn *)tableColumn;      // NSTableView

- (void)windowDidMove:(NSNotification *)notification;            // NSWindow

- (void)application:(UIApplication *)application

    willChangeStatusBarFrame:(CGRect)newStatusBarFrame;            // UIApplication

- (void)applicationWillBecomeActive:(NSNotification *)notification;   // NSApplication
```
There are a couple of things to note about this last group of methods. The first is that an auxiliary verb of "Will" (as in the third method) does not necessarily mean that a return value is expected. In this

case, the event is imminent and cannot be blocked, but the message gives the delegate an opportunity to prepare the program for the event.

The other point of interest concerns the second and last method declarations in Listing 3-2 . The sole parameter of each of these methods is an NSNotificationobject, which means that these methods are invoked as the result of the posting of a particular notification. For example, the windowDidMove: method is associated with
the NSWindow notification NSWindowDidMoveNotification. It's important to understand the relationship of notifications to delegation messages in AppKit. The delegating object automatically makes its delegate an observer of all notifications it posts. All the delegate needs to do is implement the associated method to get the notification.

To make an instance of your custom class the delegate of an AppKit object, simply connect the instance to the delegate outlet or property in Interface Builder. Or you can set it programmatically through the delegating object's setDelegate: method or delegate property, preferably early on, such as in the awakeFromNib orapplicationDidFinishLaunching: method.

Delegation and the Application Frameworks

The delegating object in a Cocoa or Cocoa Touch application is often a responder object such as a UIApplication, NSWindow, or NSTableView object. The delegate object itself is typically, but not necessarily, an object, often a custom object, that controls some part of the application (that is, a coordinating controller object). The following AppKit classes define a delegate:

- NSApplication
- NSBrowser
- NSControl
- NSDrawer
- NSFontManager
- NSFontPanel
- NSMatrix
- NSOutlineView
- NSSplitView
- NSTableView
- NSTabView
- NSText

- `NSTextField`
- `NSTextView`
- `NSWindow`

The UIKit framework also uses delegation extensively and always implements it using formal protocols. The application delegate is extremely important in an application running in iOS because it must respond to application-launch, application-quit, low-memory, and other messages from the application object. The application delegate must adopt the UIApplicationDelegate protocol.

Delegating objects do not (and should not) retain their delegates. However, clients of delegating objects (applications, usually) are responsible for ensuring that their delegates are around to receive delegation messages. To do this, they may have to retain the delegate in memory-managed code. This precaution applies equally to data sources, notification observers, and targets of action messages. Note that in a garbage-collection environment, the reference to the delegate is strong because the retain-cycle problem does not apply.

Some AppKit classes have a more restricted type of delegate called a modal delegate. Objects of these classes (NSOpenPanel, for example) run modal dialogs that invoke a handler method in the designated delegate when the user clicks the dialog's OK button. Modal delegates are limited in scope to the operation of the modal dialog.

Becoming the Delegate of a Framework Class

A framework class or any other class that implements delegation declares a delegate property and a protocol (usually a formal protocol). The protocol lists the required and optional methods that the delegate implements. For an instance of your class to function as the delegate of a framework object, it must do the following:

- Set your object as the delegate (by assigning it to the delegate property). You can do this programmatically or through Interface Builder.

- If the protocol is formal, declare that your class adopts the protocol in the class definition.

  For example: @interface MyControllerClass : UIViewController <UIAlertViewDelegate> {

- Implement all required methods of the protocol and any optional methods that you want to participate in.

Locating Objects Through the delegate Property

The existence of delegates has other programmatic uses. For example, with delegates it is easy for two coordinating controllers in the same program to find and communicate with each other. For example, the object controlling the application overall can find the controller of the application's inspector window (assuming it's the current key window) using code similar to the following:

id winController = [[NSApp keyWindow] delegate];

And your code can find the application-controller object—by definition, the delegate of the global application instance—by doing something similar to the following:

id appController = [NSApp delegate];

Data Sources

A data source is like a delegate except that, instead of being delegated control of the user interface, it is delegated control of data. A data source is an outlet held byNSView and UIView objects such as table views and outline views that require a source from which to populate their rows of visible data. The data source for a view is usually the same object that acts as its delegate, but it can be any object. As with the delegate, the data source must implement one or more methods of an informal protocol to supply the view with the data it needs and, in more advanced implementations, to handle data that users directly edit in such views.

As with delegates, data sources are objects that must be present to receive messages from the objects requesting data. The application that uses them must ensure their persistence, retaining them if necessary in memory-managed code.

Data sources are responsible for the persistence of the objects they hand out to user-interface objects. In other words, they are responsible for the memory management of those objects. However, whenever a view object such as an outline view or table view accesses the data from a data source, it retains the objects as long as it uses the data. But it does not use the data for very long. Typically it holds on to the data only long enough to display it.

Implementing a Delegate for a Custom Class

To implement a delegate for your custom class, complete the following steps:

Declare the delegate accessor methods in your class header file.

- (id)delegate;

- (void)setDelegate:(id)newDelegate;

Implement the accessor methods. In a memory-managed program, to avoid retain cycles, the setter method should not retain or copy your delegate.

- (id)delegate {

   return delegate;

}

- (void)setDelegate:(id)newDelegate {

   delegate = newDelegate;

}

In a garbage-collected environment, where retain cycles are not a problem, you should not make the delegate a weak reference (by using the __weak type modifier). For more on retain cycles, see Advanced Memory Management Programming Guide. For more on weak references in garbage collection, see Garbage Collection for Cocoa Essentials in Garbage Collection Programming Guide.

Declare a formal or informal protocol containing the programmatic interface for the delegate. Informal protocols are categories on the NSObject class. If you declare a formal protocol for your delegate, make sure you mark groups of optional methods with the @optional directive.

The Form of Delegation Messages gives advice for naming your own delegation methods.

Before invoking a delegation method, make sure the delegate implements it by sending it a respondsToSelector: message.

```
- (void)someMethod {

    if ( [delegate respondsToSelector:@selector(operationShouldProceed)] ) {

        if ( [delegate operationShouldProceed] ) {

            // do something appropriate

        }

    }

}
```

The precaution is necessary only for optional methods in a formal protocol or methods of an informal protocol.

Chapter 5: Creating User Interface

To unleash the power of OS X, you develop apps using the Cocoa application environment. Cocoa presents the app's user interface and integrates it tightly with the other components of the operating system. Cocoa provides an integrated suite of object-oriented software components packaged in two core class libraries, the AppKit and Foundation frameworks, and a number of underlying frameworks providing supporting technologies. Cocoa classes are reusable and extensible—you can use them as is or extend them for your particular requirements.

Cocoa makes it easy to create apps that adopt all of the conventions and expose all of the power of OS X. In fact, you can create a new Cocoa application project in Xcode and, without adding any code, have a functional app. Such an app is able to display its window (or create new documents) and implements many standard system behaviors. And although the Xcode templates provide some code to make this all happen, the amount of code they provide is minimal. Most of the behavior is provided by Cocoa itself.

To make a great app, you should build on the foundations Cocoa lays down for you, working with the conventions and infrastructure provided for you. To do so effectively, it's important to understand how a Cocoa app fits together.

5.1 Exploring XIB File

Let's explore what we find in a typical XIB user interface file, just so we can start to explore some of the other controls. I will make a brand new project, and I'm just going to go into the MainMenu.xib file and to make sure that I can see my Utilities panel, so I can get to myLibraries and Inspectors. We have seen that we have the Dock area over here on the left of the canvas which can be maximized or minimized, but not hidden. And it has two main sections inside it, what are called Placeholders and Objects.

Now, the Placeholders represent shortcuts to important objects, and often objects outside of this actual user interface file. So in the Placeholders section I see File's Owner, First Responder, and Application. And you will always see these three placeholders in every Cocoa user interface. The easy one is application. It represents the running application object itself. Now, we won't do much with this icon in this ebook, but it's good to have a visual representation of the actual app.

For example, if I drill into the standard menu that's generated for a new Cocoa application, we have got the menu that's being generated for the project itself, which includes the Quit option. We will go into the menus in more detail, but just if I were to right-click on that, I could actually see that like having a button or some other control, it can send actions, it can be an outlet and right now this is set up to send the terminate action to the Application object. And if you notice, as I mouse over application, it's actually highlighting up there in the Placeholder.

So it can be useful to be able to grab hold of something that represents that application object. Well, what about the other two? Well File's Owner, is an icon that represents a connection from this user interface file to the object that owns it that was responsible for loading it. Now here, this MainMenu.xib is actually loaded by the NSApplication object because this part of the interface lives as long as the application lives. So here File's Owner and the Application Placeholder both point to the same thing, but that's not always the case. If we were to create another window that didn't need to live as long, say our Preferences panel, it could have adifferent File's Owner.

And the last one is First Responder. This is a somewhat cryptic name. This is a placeholder that can represent different objects at different times in the application lifecycle. But it refers to the fact that there's always one object in the UI that should get the first opportunity to respond to an event. As a very basic example, say we have been manipulating this interface, and wehave dragged on a couple of text fields. Well, if you click into a text field, that text field that you have just selected, should now be the thing that responds to key presses.

But if you click into a different text field, it should be the First Responder to those key presses. So sometimes it's useful to be able to ask who is the current First Responder or even set a First Responder programmatically, and we will see more about this later. But we have got the main section here below that, the Objects section, and there are far more of these, mostly representing visual user interface elements on our canvas, but can be non-visual too. Because this is an Apple operating system, we have two primary sections set up for us in a basic Cocoa application.

The Main Menu object, which itself contains a collection of Menu Items and other menus, and the Window object itself, these things are both contained in the user interface file, but they are separate chunks. And Ofcourse, Objects can contain other objects. Beyond the most basic interaction, it is useful to have the expanded view of the Dock rather than the minimized view of the Dock when you're looking at this. So I can click the disclosure triangle and start to drill down into the different sections inside, for example, the Menu.

Selecting any of these objects should highlight it correctly on the actual screen and the reverse is true as well. You can treat the menu as a menu to be able to drill down into optional settingsinside it, and you will find that each individual piece of the menu is essentially its own separate object. Selecting any particular entry from any particular part of the menu allows us to look at that individual piece such as Show Toolbar, I could use the Connections Inspector, see if it has any actions or outlets and just treat it completely independently of other menu items.

Some of these menu items, you'll find, are hooked up such as the Quit option in the main application menu. Right-clicking or using the Connections Inspector, we can see that that'ssending the terminate action to the Application object. Others say Preferences might be very common, but right-clicking that one I can see that might be there, but it's hooked up to nothing yet. And that would be our job to do this to create say a Preferences window. Below the Menu section we have the main Window section, which itself contains a view, this main visible area that we can drag and drop buttons and text fields and other controls onto.

And we will see a lot more about what we can do with this view in the next few movies. Below this are a couple of non-visual objects meaning, just objects. These represent an object, an instance of a class, like the App Delegate represents an instance of the AppDelegate class that's written in our project. And we have seen this one already. Having it here visually you know our XIB file allows us to connect to it and to call certain methods inside it. We also have, in our basic Cocoa application, the Font Manager. This is a built-in Cocoa object that's provided here by Xcode so that the standard font menu inside Format can have an object to talk to.

And we can just ignore Font Manager for now. But here's the question. What is Xcode actually doing when we say drag on a button from the Object Library? What does it do here? On many, perhaps most IDEs, when you work with a visual user interface design like this, it's actually generating programmatic code behind the scenes. It might be generating lines of Java, or C#, or VB.NET. That are instantiating objects and setting their X and Y positions based where you drag them on the window.

Well, this is not the way that Xcode works. When we start arranging different buttons and controls on the screens are working with the menus, it's not generating Objective-C, or C, or C++, or any other procedural language. A XIB file, behind the scenes, is made of XML. It's not procedural, it's like an XML snapshot of all the objects the way you have arranged them and the attributes you have set on them, the things that you have connected them to. If I right-click this MainMenu.xib file in Xcode, I can choose to open it as source code, and I actually see that it is just seriously a list of XML in different settings about how the menu is created, what objects have been dragged on, and information about those objects.

You do not need to edit the XML, as a rule you just stay in Interface Builder, so to get back to that I just told it to open as Interface Builder. So whatever we do, whatever we arrange, whatever we change in an XIB file is basically saved in a snapshot of XML. You will often hear the term freeze-dried for this, but when you arrange and save this XIB file, it's like having a bunch of objects frozen in place. And when that XIB is loaded, everything is unfrozen, or reconstituted, exactly how you define the interface in Xcode.

But what we are going to do in the next section is explore more of what we can do with a user interface in Cocoa, talk about some of the most common controls you are likely to use from the Object Library, how to lay out an interface well, make it flexible, and some user interface conventions in Cocoa that you may be aware of and a few you may not, but you should be. So I won't be writing a great deal of code in the next few movies until we have seen what we can do by just using the visual options.

5.2 Working with Buttons

The first time you create a new Cocoa application and you open up the Object Library to see your available user interface elements, there looks like there's a tremendous amount of things here to choose from, and it's true there are a lot, but not quite as many as it might seem. For a little bit more information on any of them, you can select them, then hover the mouse, you'll get a pop-up that tells you a little bit more information about that particular control. And this is what I mean by saying there is not quite as many controls as it might seem.

The first bunch here, for example, are all exactly the same class, the NSButton class. In fact, I have to come down 14 entries to find something that isn't an NSButton. And in fact, NSButton is actually a really good place to start when we want to get familiar with the Cocoa controls. So let's see a few of them. I'm going to jump into my MainMenu.xib file here and just select the Window object. Drag on a few of the basic buttons here. We have got a Push button, Gradient button, Rounded Rect button, I won't do every single one, but I'll have a few of them.

Textured button, Disclosure Triangle, and let's go with a Square button. They're all based on the same underlying class, although they obviously look substantially different. If I open up my Inspector section and go to my Attributes Inspector, which is the fourth Inspectors Panel here, I can actually see that each button has a style, and it looks like I could change this from say a Square button to a Push button, to a Disclosure Triangle and back. But I would say that if you accidentally dragged on the wrong kind, and you haven't hooked it up to anything yet. Don't just ever change the style.

Delete the button, go back and drag on the one you wanted because there is a lot more to a button than style, as we'll see in a moment. But this Attributes Inspector is, in fact, a great way to get an idea of the options for these buttons and for any controls. Though for more on each control, with it selected, selecting the second Inspector will give you the Quick Help menu. Now, the first abstract here doesn't give you more than you can get just by clicking in the Object Library and waiting for the pop-up, but you also have a link here to say the NSButton Class Reference, which will jump us to the Documentation and tell us the kind of things we could do in code, giving us an idea of what this button is capable of. Apparently we can set the sound on it, we can set it to Transparent. It's got things like bezelStyle.

Switching back to the main environment, there is also a link to a guide called button Programming Topics, although this at least at the time of recording for Apple is surprisingly out of date. So let's go back and take a look at a few of these. I'm going to switch back into my Attributes Inspector. Many buttons have, as we can see, a Title. You can double-click in here to change it to something else, or Ofcourse, you can change it in the Attributes Inspector, which will do the same thing. But several buttons, a Square button, for example, does not have a title, even though there is a space for one.

You can add one, or you can give a button an image instead of, or in addition to, a title. But if a button doesn't have a title when dragged on, it can be a clue that this kind of button is expected to have an image. So with the Square button selected I can see that I do have a dropdown Image section here in the Attributes Inspector, and just by clicking that I'm going tosee several entries. What we're looking at here are some of the official Apple button and Toolbar images. We have got ColorPanel here, we have got Computer, we have got the images for Everyone, we have got the images for DotMac and Advanced settings.

However, just because you can select an image here, doesn't mean you should. Some of these are only supposed to be used in Toolbars, and most of them really do represent a very specific meaning for Apple. So you don't want to use, for example, NSUserGroup for your button thinking that might be a good icon for chat, when in fact this is a very specific Apple icon meant to be used for user group permissions. Now, your question might be, well, how am I supposed to know which one of these I can use and which ones I can't and in what circumstances? Well, bear with me, we will get to that.

Ofcourse, what's often likely is that you'll want to have your own images for icons. Now, unlike some platforms, including iOS, there is no one particular size that you must provide for a button icon because buttons can be large, they can be tiny, they can be anywhere in between.But a Square PNG file is best with a transparent background. I have one on my Desktop at the moment, what I'm going to do is just add it to this project. I'll click the Supporting Files folder because that's usually where I'd want this to be, and in Xcode I could just drag and drop this, but I can also go to File and then Add Files to this project, the project is called buttons.

I'll go and find this, it should be on my Desktop. I have something called SimpleImage. It's just a PNG, a very small file here. With that selected, I want to check the box to say Copy this item into the destination group folder, to make sure I'm not just linking to it on the Desktop, but I'll keep it in my Project folder, click OK, and now I can see SimpleImage.png, very straightforward turn up there. Switching back into the interface, what I should now be able to do with that button selected is go over here into the dropdown Image, and I should find it show up in the list. There we go, SimpleImage.

Now, the most common thing Ofcourse to do with a button is hook it up to some code, meaning cause an action. A button that doesn't cause an action isn't really all that useful. Now, we have seen this already, but let's just take another look at it again. I'll give myself a bit more screen real estate here and switch into my Assistant Editor mode. We want to see the AppDelegate over here. I could create a new class, but just for the purposes of a quick demo this is fine. I'm looking at the header file. I'm going to Ctrl-drag from any of these buttons in here to insert an action.

The pop-up, by default it pops up as Outlet. buttons can be both Outlets and Actions, but it's certainly more common that they're all actions. I'll call this doSomething. We have now connected that button up to this little piece of code. But while all of my buttons are likely to cause actions. oftentimes I'll want to also talk to the button in code, I'll want to change its title or set it from Enabled to Disabled. Now, to talk to a specific button directly in code, it's useful to define that button as an Outlet and give that Outlet a name.

So, for example, I'm going to select this Gradient button here. Ctrl-drag that into the interface. I prefer to put all my properties before my methods, it doesn't really matter what order the properties are in. So this on the other hand, is not an action, it's an Outlet, and I'll give it aname of myGradientButton. It's of Type NSButton, that looks correct, and it's weak, there we go. The reason that I wanted to do this is to show what's probably the second most common thing to do with a button. If the first is hook it up and make it cause an action, the second most common thing is to make a button enabled or disabled.

Now, this can be done in the Interface Builder, so if I have my Utilities Panel open, I can select that Gradient button and down towards the bottom here we have a check box here called Enabled. If I uncheck that, we immediately see the different visual style over here in the Interface that suggests we can't click this button. But we often want to do that too in code. We want to affect whether a button is enabled or disabled in code. So what I'm going to do now is switch to the Implementation and turn that button back on.

Because we have defined it as an Outlet called myGradientButton, I can just use the name of that. myGradientButton has a method called setEnabled, and it's a BOOL, which for Objective-C is YES. Alternatively, I could have used dot syntax here, myGradientButton.Enabled = YES.Save that and Run it. The application should begin with the button Disabled, but not surprisingly we click the first Push button, and we should get the option to Enable it.

5.3 Exploring the Apple Human Interface Guidelines for OS X

If you have been using a Mac for a while, several of the button choices in the Cocoa Application are pretty obvious. You can tell the difference between say using a Push button, and when you might use something like a Disclosure button. However, most developers even with long histories on the Mac are less sure when the question is something like when should you use a Gradient button as opposed to a Square button as opposed to a Bevel button? What's the difference between using a Recessed button and an Inline button, particularly as they look almost identical in the Library section? And Ofcourse, this is Apple, so we can presume that all these choices matter, it's not arbitrary.

Well, we need to step up our knowledge of Apple's official Human Interface Guidelines. Now this is a document that you can get from the Apple developer site. And if I go into the Mac Dev Center, I often don't even need to be logged in to be able to find it. I'm going to jump into the Guides section of the Mac OS X Developer Library. It's usually fairly obvious somewhere on this page, but if not, you can Ofcourse search for it.

This is what I'm looking for, the Mac OS X Human Interface Guidelines. There are actually separate documents for OS X and iOS development. You can get this document on the web, but you can also download a PDF version of it if you prefer to put it on a reader or print it out.PDF is over 300 pages, but this is not your usual dry technical documentation, it's not primarily about code, and it is written very, very well. Over here on the left-hand side I can see it is split up into several sections.

We go to section on the basics of the Mac OS X platform, there's some high-level content like the Philosophy of User Interface Design. Everything from Consistency, Forgiveness, and Aesthetic Integrity, but it also gets into very specific low- level content like Designing icons for the Sidebar or the Toolbar. And there are two sections certainly worth becoming very familiar with early on. If I come down to the sections here that talk about the User Interface Element Guidelines, I'm going to select the Windows section here.

And if you want to make sure that you're good with the differences between a window, a document, a panel, an alert and a sheet, this is going to break it down, give you a nice quick reference for that. It will break down some of the terminology that you will read in Apple documentation, talking about say the window-frame area, the title bar and the toolbar, the window-body, because what you'll find is a lot of buttons and different elements are suggested that they only exist in the window-frame or they only exist in the window-body. What this document is great for is making explicit what is often only implicit when you have just been a Mac user.

After you have gotten familiar with the Window Guidelines, take a look at the User Interface Element Guidelines for Controls. Here is where you'll find very specific guidelines for things like button usage. There is an entire section on Window-Frame Controls. Again, if you're looking at something that appears in the toolbar that kind of button there, if it's a separate button the suggestion being it's a Round textured button. If the visual appearance is something like this the four groups together you're looking at the Textured rounded segmented control.

It will break down the differences between pop-up menus and pop-down menus. So when you're asking which button should I use in which circumstance? This is a great part of the document to get to. In fact, if you jump into the buttons section, it will break down guidelines on when Push buttons should be used. As you read this document, you'll find the guidelines on things like if one of these buttons is going to pop-up another dialog box, then you should have be ellipses after it. As we come down further this guidelines about when to use Icon buttons, whatsize you should be working with, there.

Scope buttons, recessed scope buttons versus round rectangle scope buttons. Again, all of the things we kind of take for granted using the Mac that we now have to make explicit as Cocoa Developers. An example of when to use a Gradient button, Gradient buttons often being used without text, using one of the built- in icons for Apple to add or subtract or work with settings and preferences. When specifically to use the Bevel button, and you'll find the Notes that they're not recommended for apps using OS v10.7 or later.

You should use a Gradient button or Segmented Control instead. Now earlier I showed examples of selecting images on a button from using some of the built-in Apple icons. Well, in Appendix B of this document you can actually find more about what images are available and exactly when they should be used. It will break down which one should only be used in Toolbars, which ones are allowed to be used in Controls. You see a preview of the image and then what you should expect that image to be called in the dropdown box. Images for locking and unlocking, going forward, going back, adding an item removing an item, they are already there, and these are the ones you should be using in Cocoa if you need that functionality.

5.4 Using Number Formatters

So if in our code we have say an NSDate object, we want it to be easy to put that directly into a text field, formatted the way we want it, without writing a lot of code to convert it, and we can use something called a formatter for that. A formatter in Cocoa changes a string into another data type or the other way around, another data type into a string.

5.5 Using The Slider Control

Jump into the MainMenu.xib file, select the window and then in the Object Library either come down to or filter on slider. We have Horizontal, Vertical, and Circular, that's something called a slider Cellbut that's really just the interior part of an NSSlider. You can drag on a horizontal one because these are the most commonly used in OS X. But they all worked the same way, and if you get familiar with one, the others hold no mystery.

Jumping over into my Attributes Inspector here, I can see that we have this idea of a Maximum and Minimum values. By default it's 0 through 100, and the Current value is 50. You can either use the stepper control here, and as you do this you should see the head of the slider is actually moving on our Design view.

You can change the Minimum and Maximum values, Ofcourse, to be anything that's meaningful for you. There is something called Tick Marks here, and you don't actually see any tick marks until you change this value to greater than zero. I am going to change it to say six here. What happens then is that the actual head--what's often called the thumb or the knob of the slider--changes from a circle to this pointer. And the tick marks are showing up, but they're positioned above by default which I find kind of odd because Apple nearly always positioned tick marks below the slider, so let's change that, Tick Marks Position Below.

And we have the choice also to only stop on the Tick Marks. Going ahead and running the application, it behaves as we'd expect to do. I am not locking to the Tick Marks, so I get a continuous movement from side to side here. But one of the best ways to figure out how they can and should be used to replicate a familiar Apple feel is go and see how Apple use them.Now if you want to see a lot of Cocoa controls in the same place quickly, there is no better place than going to System Preferences, because you can jump around in here and blast through a whole bunch of different screens that are going to show you the most commonly used Cocoa controls and how they're used.

And sure these aren't pretty conventional Cocoa screens, they are not going to win any design awards, but it is a great place to become familiar with classic usage. So if I am in Sound I can see a couple of sliders being used there. Then in the Keyboard section I see sliders being used here for Key Repeat and Delay Until Repeat. And these are typically using Tick Marks with the Tick Marks below. Now Apple suggests having labels and at at least the start and the end if you are using Tick Marks. So let's go ahead and do that. I am going to jump back into Xcode and make sure my running application is stopped and just giving myself a bit more space for this slider, drag on a couple of normal labels.

I will position one at the start and then for speed purposes just do an Option-click to put one at the end here. And change their value. Double-click that from None to Lots. They are looking a little big right now. That's because if you go to label beneath a slider it shouldn't be using the normal font. In my Attributes Inspector here I'm going to change the Font sections for this label to System Small, do that for the second one as well.

And that's more like it. Now you'll actually find switching back into System Preferences as an example that Apple usually capitalize the words being used for the certain end of tick marks but not always. Sometimes they don't. And occasionally, you'll also find some tick marks used without labels at all. Now the value of a slider should typically be enough by itself. It doesn't have to be shown anywhere else on the screen. If I'm changing this Alert value, I'm just changing the Alert value.

If I'm using a slider with a keyboard to effect the Key Repeat, it's between Slow and Fast and Off, but I don't see it updating some other piece of text that says this is 80% or 90%. But if it's helpful, you might want to do that. One example would be in the Energy Saver section of Preferences. We have a long slider here. We have several different labels being used. But as I grab the head of the slider I get this label above it kind of showing me exactly what these are pointing to. When I let go, that label disappears again.

Again this should only be done if this is useful, but I'll show you a quick way we can actually replicate that in our program with no code. I am going to go over into my Object library and just find a regular label, drag that up here above the slider. And with that label selected I am going to go over into my Connections Inspector. And so far we have seen using a Delegate connection, we have seen using Actions and Outlets, but I am going to do something else now. With the label selected I am going to come down into Received Actions where I have some interesting ones like takeFloatValueFrom from takeIntegerValueFrom.

I am going to grab the circle beside takeFloatValueFrom, click and drag over to the slider and let go. I can see the connection being taken up here. If have done it on the wrong thing I could just hit the little X to break it. I actually don't need this label to say anything, so I am just going to delete the contents of it and go ahead and run this. So grab the handle of this, move and let go, move again and let go, move again and let go.

We're partway there, but we have got a couple of issues. One is its not updating until we actually let go off the slider head. And two is it's little more information than I needed to know about the exact value of this slider. So let's fix those. Quit and back into Xcode, I am going to select the slider here. Now the first problem we were having is it was only updating when I paused, when I let go of moving the slider. I am going to jump into my Attributes Inspector, and that's because the default behavior of the slider is to only update when you let go.

But down in the Control section, if I find the check box marked Continuous and selected that, then just running this quickly again, we'll find that it updates as soon as possible, and it updates as we are dragging the slider along, but we are still getting a little bit too much information here. So back into Xcode and stop the application. I have got two methods that I could use to take care of this. First I am going to grab the label, now because it's blanked out its little difficult to grab hold of so I could use the Expanded view here. And just click around a little bit until I find the correct one which is this static text area, and I can see it being highlighted.

Well, one thing that I could do is in the Connections Inspector instead of hooking that up to takeFloatValueFrom, I could cancel that and then just hook it up to takeIntValueFrom. And that would just truncate that value, which would work fine. Another way we could do seeing as we're working with a format as recently is I could find the Number Formatter, just drag that on top of the label. It's not letting me do that right now because it's a bit too empty to drag on top of.

So let me highlight that static text field and just give it a simple bit of text here so I actually have something to grab hold of. Drag on the Number Formatter, let go. And then we can blank out that value again and run. We have the slider, as soon as I click it and drag down we have the Integer value. I might change the alignment of that, but it's working just fine.

And what I wanted to demonstrate by doing this is the ability as we get more and more aware of the different controls in Cocoa that's very common to connect them to each other. To have one control directly affect another without having to write any code at all. Now in Code if I wanted to get the value of the slider, I could set it up as an IB outlet, give it a name, and then use the floatValue property to get its current value as a float, or the Int value to get as an Int, or String value to get as a string. And you might be thinking, oh, so NSSlider has a String value property just like NSText field? Well, yes it does because they all do.

Every control has those same properties, Int value, Float value, String value, Object value and many more besides, because all of the controls we have been using and all of the ones you'll find here that you can drag and drop onto the screen end up inheriting from a class called NSControl, selecting the Classic Controls here, everything like a Gradient button or a Push button. If I let the pop-up come up, it will tell me it's a subclass of NSControl. The Text field is a subclass of NSControll or kind of NSControl, as are the rest of them even say a secure text field inherits from NSText field which itself inherits from an NSControl.

Chapter 6: Arranging User Interface

6.1 Using Layout Views

As we begin to make interfaces with more controls and more choices on them, we need to start organizing some of those controls, or at least making it explicit which ones belong together. And when you first start building Cocoa Applications it is a really good idea to keep in mind some of the things that Apple do and some of the precedents that they set, whether you're looking at things like iWork Applications or even just the good old System Preferences.

I'll give you some ideas about what might we expected in an Apple environment. That will give you everything from say the basic General section in System Preferences which simply uses some horizontal lines to separate some Radio buttons and check boxes and a few of these controls what are called Pop-up buttons that we haven't really explored yet.

If I jump back in and go over to the preferences for Mission Control, we'll see these ones here just having several control like these check boxes inside a box, and in fact, that is what this is called in Cocoa is just a Box, it's a way of grouping some controls together and optionally giving them a name like this Keyboard and Mouse Shortcuts box. Jumping over to Desktop & Screen Saver, we have the first of many what are called Tab Views, where we have two or three or four clickable links at the top of this window. I'll jump to Security & Privacy. I have four different Tab views, each one containing an independent collection of controls.

And Keyboard, for example, we have just a couple of sliders, some labels, check boxes, and regular buttons. And in the second Tab, Keyboard Shortcuts, we have something this little more complex here. We have something called a Split view that separating these two sections, allowing me to resize the amount that I see. Now while we have seen buttons and check boxes and sliders, we haven't seen these controls yet. We're going to explore these in the next chapter, the ones with the lists of selections. What I'm focused on right now on the Containers themselves, the Dividers, things like the Tab Views and the Boxes and everything that I have just mentioned Horizontal Lines, Vertical Lines, Boxes, Tab views, Split Views all the typicalways to contain surround and set out controls inside the same window. These are all the available for us to drag and drop in Interface Builder there in the Object Library in a section called Layout Views.

There's eight of them here, ranging from the very simple to just being able to drag on say a Vertical Line and resize that, to more complex like the Vertical Split view or Horizontal Split view. Going to just delete that vertical line and drag on a couple of things to help me set out this window. First I'll drag on a Tab view here. I'll use the guidelines to help me laid out. And with the Tab view itself selected, I can see that we start off with two tabs. It's invisible on the page. It's visible here in my Attributes Inspector.

I can change that to three or to four. I do want to be careful because each individual tab will switch my focus here, so if I click on the word Tab again, we're actually jumping into that first tab which will allow me to drag and drop different controls here. So this is occasionally where it's useful to expand the Dock to allow me to select the Tab view itself rather than the independent pieces, what are I refer to as the Tab view Item, which themselves are very useful to use such is the second item, the third, or the fourth.

Selecting any of them allows me to drag on the regular controls or even other views. The Push buttons, Labels, Text Fields, and so on. And each of these are completely independent, supported both in your program when it runs and in Interface Builder itself. If I click the second tab twice we'll shift into that mode, and I can drag on some new content here. In this case perhaps Date Pickers and a Combo Box or two. Now if necessary, one of the things you can also do is have containers inside containers.

I could switch back to my Layout view section here and decide to drag a Box into that second tab. Now if I made up my mind that what I really I wanted to have was these three controls inside that box, well I could move them across, but another way to do it is use the Command key and select all three of those, and I want to be sure it's just those three selected. And come up to the Editor section and say Embed In > Box. And that gives me the Box with just those three controls. And if you notice, that as I move the box around those are considered enclosed in it.

And that's the way you'll see them over here in the expanded Dock. Just collapsing some of these disclosure triangles to make it a bit more obvious, we have the Tab view which itself includes the separate items, but if I select the second item and expand that, we have the view inside that that contains two boxes. One of the boxes itself can be expanded, and that contains the Combo Box directly. The thing you have to be careful of here is if you're rearranging an Interface I don't want to select the Box--I'm thinking I can delete it without deleting what's inside it because if I do hit the Delete key it all goes away, including all of its contents.

So I'll just Command+Z here to bring that back. But Ofcourse the Tab view that I'm looking at here is completely independent of whatever else is happening on that window. So if we drag on the Box underneath it, and I can double-click the name of that just to give it a new name, or you can set it to blank if you want to. Just to quickly drag on the couple of things, if I did expect to create say a few Text Fields and a few Labels at the same time, one quick way of doing that is coming down and finding what's called a form which begins by adding two at a time.

Though, if you have more space you can actually increase that to three or four or however many you need. I'm going to bring that back down to two rows. Now just quickly running this, we have no code whatsoever, nothing has been hooked on, no outlets, no actions. But it's very easy to start to set this out and just start to emulate some of the kind of presentation styles that you'd see in say System Preferences. The last thing that I wanted to show was in that Layout view section, the Split view. I'm going to select the third tab which right now for me is blank.

We can drag one of these on--say a Vertical Split view--and position that, arrange it, resize it.Right now, the individual sections inside the say Custom view have nothing in them whatsoever. We can drag our own controls in to it if we want to. But what's more usual is that you use a Split view in conjunction with a couple of the controls we haven't really explored yet, most of which are found in Data Views, such as the Browser and the Outline view that are showing lists of content. It's unusual that we'd use a movable Split view and have just buttons and check boxes on either side of it.

And while I could drag and drop in a Table view or Outline, we can actually use the same technique that we used on the second view here with embedding controls inside another one.So I'm going to jump to that fourth tab, and just ignoring the Split view completely, I'll drag on first a Browser. Browser we'll see a little later. That's something that you might use and say a Finder window, and then after this I'm going to grab a Table view just to have a different control to work with.

I'll drag that into that tab as well. Now if I decide what I want it once to have a Split view between these two, I really need to combine them together. So I'm going to select the second one--which is the Table view--then use my Command key and select the first one. And again go up to Editor > Embed In and one of the choices here is Split view. Things about it for a second and gives us that. We may need to resize some that content, as you can see. Just to make it little more even, I can Ofcourse still get to each individual font.

If I expand this Split view I'll see that it shows me it's containing both the first Browser here and the Table view. So I'm just going to go ahead and Run this, and I can see up at the top I have this scrollable Split view here. We can switch to one which has no content in either end. We have got the boxes, we have got the regular controls. So in just a few moments, pretty easy to see how we can emulate something that we'd see in, say, System Preferences. But one thing that is actually missing between that and a typical System Preferences is the Toolbar, a very common thing in OS X Applications, and we'll see how to work with those in a moment.

6.2 Exploring Auto Layout

In 2011 Apple released AutoLayout, a new method for how Cocoa user interfaces arrange and resize and lay themselves out. Now AutoLayout replaces the older technique called Struts and Springs, which is still currently what you used in iOS development. And with Xcode 4.3, AutoLayout became the default layout method for Cocoa projects. And I am in 4.4 now, and it's what we are going to be using in this ebook. I won't be talking about the older Struts and Springs methods. Now we have been using AutoLayout already, and a lot of the time it just works.

It's worthwhile to know a little bit more about what's going on. So I have just created a new out-of- the-box Cocoa application, haven't done anything to it yet. I am going to drag on a button or two. Now we have seen the guidelines that appear when you do this. And let me tell you that AutoLayout is not at all about these guidelines, and it's not really even about the button, it's about what happens when you let go. We see the guidelines here on the left and on the top, the dotted blue lines, but if I let go you'll see another couple of lines appear, in this case to the top and to the left. This is what AutoLayout is all about.

These are what are referred to as Constraints. And Constraints describe a relationship between two visual elements, two views, like the relationship between the button and the top of the window here or the relationship between the button and the left-hand side of the window. If I click on the button over here on the right, I see two different constraints again to the top but this time to the right. As I'm dragging on different elements onto the page, different constraints are added depending on which part of the window that I put them on.

Oftentimes those constraints are based on say the right-hand or left-hand side of the window, but if I'm trying to arrange buttons beside each other, say down here, for example, I will also get constraints between the user interface elements themselves. So this selected button doesn't have a constraint to the right-hand side of the window, but it does have a constraint to the button next to it. And depending on the circumstance, a constraint might try and keep things together or keep things apart or both at the same time, in this case keep these buttons close but never allow them to touch.

Well, Constraints aren't actual objects and Cocoa, it's the NSLayout constraint object. They are added by Interface Builder as we edit our XIB files. So if you click any of the objects, whether they are buttons or any other kind of user interface elements, you'll then see the constraints that affect that object. For this one now I have three constraints, the right-hand, the bottom, and the one to the next button. You can then actually click any one of these constraints. Sometimes they are a little difficult to grab hold of, but you can usually manage.

When you click that constraint, you'll see an amber highlight that will show you what objects that constraint affects, so this one between the two affects these two buttons, this constraint just affects this button. Now as a side note it's a common mistake for new Cocoa developers to accidentally have a constraint selected when they think they have a button or some other element selected. So if you see the amber highlight, know that you have a constraint selected, you don't want to be trying to Ctrl-drag from a constraint to a code file. When buttons are properly selected they should be blue.

You can also get to constraints from the expanded Dock view. So here, for example, inside the Main view I can see the different constraints I have and actually take turns and selecting different ones vertical space, horizontal space, and so on. These are true objects. With any one of them selected, I actually have elements in the Attributes Inspector that I can affect, and we'll see this in a moment. Now most of the time you don't add constraint yourself, you just let Xcode do it. But occasionally you can, occasionally it's needed and worthwhile.

6.3 Adding and Editing Toolbars

Now the Toolbar itself doesn't have a lot of options. If I have it selected and look at my Attributes Inspector, I get a choice here of whether to show the Icon and Label or just the Icon or just the Label, but other than that, there is not really a lot going on here. So I'll leave at the default state of Icon and Label. The first request of most people is how do I add something to it? Now I have seen people try and quickly say drag and drop things like a Push button onto the Toolbar. That is not going to work and has no effect at all.

First, you need to be editing the Toolbar correctly, and you do this slightly differently from most of the things we have seen so far. So if the Toolbar is deselected, click it to select it, and if nothing pops up, click it again. You're looking for this, the Toolbar Editing Sheet. This is how you make any changes to the Toolbar. And again, just to show that's usually from a deselected state, you need to select the Toolbar then click it again to pop up the sheet. So there is two sections to this.

What is Allowed on the Toolbar and below that what is the Default arrangement of these icons, because Cocoa supports user- driven customization of the Toolbar, so an application can have many more options available than just the one shown when they open the app for the first time.So the lower section is what describes what we currently see on the user interface and what arrangement it has. And we can delete from the lower section to change that, you'll just drag off. So I'll grab the Fonts, drag out of that square, and let go, and we get the little puff cloud.

The Font option is still there, but it's no longer on the shown Toolbar. So to add new items to the toolbar, you first need to add them to the top area so they become Allowed Toolbar Items. What do you add? Well, you actually can add just a regular Push button. I see the plus sign there, but I'm not going to do that, it's a bad idea. Regular Push buttons should not be added to a typical Mac style toolbar. There are specific controls we should be adding to it. One of the easiest ways is that in the Object Library here I just filter on the word Toolbar, and I'll have several options appear.

There is a handful of these, several of them are really the ones that are already there, the Print Toolbar Item, the Show Colors Toolbar Item, the Show Fonts Toolbar Item. There are three here for a Separator and Spacing, and this is probably the classic nonspecific one, the Image Toolbar Item. I'm going to drag that across into the top area and let go. This supports an image but doesn't have one yet, and it's called the Generic Label Toolbar item. With that selected, I'm going to go over into my Attributes Inspector and give it a more useful name, I'll call this one Inspect for a Label, and I'll also change its Palette Label to Inspect.

Chapter 7: Using Data Controls

7.1 Adding Data Views

We have seen a couple of controls so far like the Combo Box, where if I drag that onto a window I can then use the Attributes Inspector and manually add different items here as the list of entries. But this kind of thing is not going to work very well when we have somethingmore complex, when there's lots of data or multiple columns or data that changes all the time.So with the several controls, we need to be able to load them with data from our own objects.Everything from simple arrays to complex objects that change every time the program runs, and even while the program is running.

And you'll find these controls in the Data Views section of the Object Library. Now the first looks like there's a lot of stuff here, but most of the elements you see here are ingredients, different cells, tiny customizable pieces that fit into the larger controls. Like the first four here at the top. Right at the top is the Table view, this is the most common, most used the classic data-driven control of rows and columns of data. It starts off very basic but can be hugely customized.

A classic example might be in System Preferences in the Sound section, if we're selecting a sound effect. This is a Table view here. It's got two columns, Name and Type, so we have the headers with the name and type at the top, we can scroll up and down and select different entries on it. The Table view can be as basic as something that we would see in the Displays section, just a simple list. One column, no header, just a list of entries we can select from. Or at the other end of the scale, we could take a look at something like the App store, the list of purchase software. This could be done in a Table view too.

It's still multiple rows and multiple columns to spend more time on the presentation of each individual row. We also have the alternating lines here as well. I'm going to jumping back into Xcode. Well, if that was the Table view, what else do we have? We have here the Outline view, the Browser, and the Collection view. Here is the best way to explain these. I'm going to jump into a Finder window. Now for a second here, I'm just focused on the main section of content, forget about the left-hand side.

7.2 Adding Table Views and Data Source Classes

Table Views don't store data. These are view objects. When we have a Table view in our application, what we need is another object, a helper object that can act as that Table Views' data source. This is very similar to the idea of delegation. We are asking another object to do some work for the Table view, and then we will point the Table view to that data source.

The data source can be any class. It could even be AppDelegate, but whatever class it's going to be needs to have specific methods that answer the questions, how many rows are in this Table view and what's in each row? If you have multiple columns, it's what's in every single column of every single row? And whatever the data source answers here will be used to fuel the Table view, and we'll see this in just a second. As well as a Data Source object, the Table view often needs to be connected to a delegate object too. It uses delegation.

The delegate object needs to have methods to answer the questions, what happens if a row is selected? If anything, what happens if a row is double-clicked on to edit it? What happens if you have a plus button to add a new row or perhaps the data source itself changes to add a row or delete a row? So we're looking for very specifically named methods for both of these. Now, you could put the data source in one class and the delegate in another one, but it's very common to combine the two into a custom class.

7.3 Using Key-Value Coding

I'm going to jump now into a concept in Cocoa known as Key Value Coding, and its flipside, Key-Value Observing. And the reason why is the next feature I want to explore, Bindings, relies heavily on these, and bindings is worth the trip. Now Key-Value Coding can sound complex at first but really isn't. Although I will admit that I don't think Apple do the best job of making it accessible? Their introduction is rather wordy and short on the immediate benefits. So let me jump into this. I have got a simple project that I have created here, and I'll go through what I have done.

I have got a very straightforward new Objective-C class called Book, two strings and an integer, author, title and pageCount, about as basic as it possibly gets. And I am using Objective-C properties here, because I'm using Xcode 4.4, the getters and setters for these properties will synthesize automatically. I don't even have anything in the implementation file. So I am going to instantiate a couple of objects of this class and then on this interface I have one button that will just write an NSLog message out, very, very simple, because I want a setup to allow us to do some Key-Value Coding here.

So if I look at my AppDelegate class, all I have got here I am creating a NSMutableArray that can hold several of these book objects, and I have got a listBooks method that as we'll see is going to just write out some NSLog messages. So here's what it's doing.

In the applicationDidFinishLaunching method, I'm instantiating the NSMutableArray. Then on line 18, instantiating the firstBook object, setting its properties using the standard Objective-C methods, set author or setTitle, setPageCount.

Then on line 24, I'll add that to the allBooks MutableArray, line 26 I create another book object, and I'm using the Objective-C .syntax to set its properties just to show that we could use either way, it would have no effect whatsoever. I just wanted something here to compare and contrast. Then on line 32, we add that secondBook to the array. What I am going to do now is do some Key-Value Coding.

First, instantiate a new book called thirdBook, nothing special about that. What I am going to do next is call a method on this thirdBook object. The method I am going to call is called setValue forKey. First I will pass it a value of, I'll say "Jan Hanberg" forKey:@"author". This is Key Value Coding. We are using a string as the key to get to the property called author and then setting the value of that.

This line 36 has exactly the same impact as using the method on line 20 of setAuthor: or as the method on line 28, .author equals. We have just got a slightly different format on that. Do it again now, I am going to do it for the title. And I could go ahead and try and do this for the pageCount, which is an integer, let's say I wanted to make this 250 for the Key pageCount.

And this is the only one I'm going to have a problem with. If we want to use Key-Value Coding, the value always has to be an object. So what I need to do here, because it's complaining about this is instead of passing directly in an integer, I'm going to pass it an NSNumber thatcontains an integer. We are just wrapping that integer up. And finally, I am just going to add that to my mutable array.

7.4 Binding An Object To A User Interface

A great feature that's available to us in Cocoa that isn't available in other areas of Apple development like iOS is the idea of bindings. Binding refers to be able to connect, to bind a user interface element directly to a controller class without writing code, doing it all in the interface builder part of Xcode. So I have a Cocoa application here I'm going to use, and I have added a very simple class to it, a Book class that just exists here as a data structure. I have two NSStrings for author and title, one NSDate for the publishedDate, and an integer for pageCount.

There is nothing in the implementation of this Book class, it's just to hold some data. Now, in my AppDelegate, all I am declaring here in line 16 is a property that can hold a single instance of a book object. And in my implementation of AppDelegate, that's all I'm doing when theapplication launches is I'm instantiating that book on line 16 and setting its values on the next four lines. That's the entire setup of this. What I want to do is get the details of that object onto the interface which has nothing right now, no buttons, no fields, no secret connections.

Without bindings, what we need to do is several steps. First, we'd drag on all the user interface elements we wanted. Then we'd have to take care to connect them correctly to our chosen controller class as IBOutlets, giving them names, making sure they had the right type. And then in our controller code, we have to write code to set the values of all those outlets. If the class is complex, you often have to write quite a lot of what's referred to as glue code, or the unexciting code that purely exists to get object data into user interface elements.

Well, we are going to do something a little different here. I do need to drag on the user interface elements that I want. I am going to drag on a few labels here. Just drag this wider and give it a placeholder name. This will be the Title, drag another underneath it as Author. Technically, I don't actually need to change the values of this label. We're going to change them as soon as the program loads. And just to give us a bit of visual interest, I am selecting the first one here,and I will just make the font a little bit bigger, nothing that we haven't seen before.

This will be the point where usually I'd switch into the Assistant view and start doing the Ctrl-drag method to set them all up as IBOutlets. But that's not where we are going this time. Here is where I am going instead. I am going to select that first label, I am going to jump over here into the Bindings Inspector in my Utilities Panel. This is the second to last one. This looks like several intertwined elements or a simple Celtic knot of some kind. What I'm going to do is choose to bind the value of this label to that class that we created.

Well, the question is well, how do I do this, what am I binding to? There is a lot of options that we are seeing. Well, the question is what class contains the data? Well, it's in the AppDelegate. That's what instantiates that object and holds onto it. So I am going to check the box to Bind to and then from the dropdown, select AppDelegate. But Ofcourse there is quite a lot going on in AppDelegate, so I have got a little exclamation mark here highlighting that this is the important part. We might be binding this label to the AppDelegate, but what part of the AppDelegate? And this is where we're using the term key.

We are using the key part of the key value coding which is what allows us to do a path that drills down through multiple objects. So, self refers to AppDelegate. Then I put a dot, and it's actually looking inside AppDelegate and saying, okay, I know about two properties you have. There is the window property and singleBook. Well, it's inside that singleBook property. So I will select that and hit Tab. But that's the entire class, so it knows it can't bind that yet. I'm still getting the exclamation mark. I'll hit the dot again, and it's looking inside the singleBook object saying these are the accessible properties, the NSString for Author and Title, the Date, and the pageCount.

7.5 Binding More Complex Controls

For simple binding examples, we can bind directly to an object declared in the app delegate, as we just did. But as we get more advanced, that won't be good enough. Now first realize the role that I'm talking about here. We are still doing Model-view controller. We have go the user interface view object, something even as simple as a text field. We have go to model, the actual data, and with the bindings, we can minimize a lot of the glue code in the middle and the controller, but we can't, and we don't want to remove it from the picture, it's still a vital part.

So in that previous simple example, we still went through the AppDelegate as the Controller to act as a middleman between the user interface view Objects and the Model Object, in this case, one Book object, and again, there was nothing in the Book object that knew anything about a user interface element. So it's this bit in the middle I'm talking about here, the Controller. We have already seen earlier in the ebook that yes, we can use the AppDelegate as a controller. We can create a regular Objective-C class to act in the role of controller.

But there are several classes built into Cocoa to help us in the role of controller when we're using bindings. In a more complex situation where we have complex view objects like table views that we want to use, and complex model objects, arrays, dictionaries, objects that contain other objects. We need to ask a few more questions about what's in the middle. And the key question we need when choosing between the options is first, what kind of data do you have? What is your model? Is your model object a single object? Is it a collection, like an array or dictionary? Is it a complex tree of objects with parents and children? Because we have some choices about what we can put in the middle, in the controller role.

For single objects, we have something built into Cocoa called the Object Controller, NSObjectController class. If you have an array, we have an Array Controller, we have a Dictionary Controller, and even a Tree Controller for complex trees of objects. And using these in the controller role can make binding these complex controls much easier. What they do is stand between the user interface view object and our model, our data, helping us not just blind, but sort and add and edit and delete.

But how do you use these? One easy way is that they are already there in Xcode. If I go into my Object Library, into the Objects and Controller section, I will find them listed here. Notice the description here, Object Controller is a Cocoa bindings compatible controller class. Bindings Compatible Controller class, Bindings Compatible Controller class for the Object, Array, Dictionary and Tree Controllers. There's even a User Defaults Controller to allow us to bind to the user defaults in OS X. Now these on non- visual Objects, but we can drag them on to the Dock, like dragging on the blue object box that we have done a couple of times earlier.

In this way connect them between on model objects and our user interface view objects. Now there's a common misconception I sometimes hear, and I want to clear up. Is that some people come in to this thinking you can only have one controller object per window that you must choose what is the controller object. And that's not true, you can have as many as you need. Now I occasionally hear this from people who are used to working with MVC where it's formalized a certain way, even in iOS, where it's very common to have one controller per view, one controller object dealing with all the user interface elements on a particular screen.

And that method can work very well, but MVC does not force you to do it that way. Think about it this way, you can have way more than one view object on this window. We know that. We can have text boxes and buttons and text views. In fact, the window itself is a view object. A menu is, a menu item is, and we know they we can have more than one model object. We could have an array of books, an array of authors, complex classes being used on this one screen. In the same way we could have more than one controller if it helps.

7.6 Using Nsarraycontroller with Table Views

Now let's see how to connect more complex objects to more complex user interface elements. I have a simple project that I have created to get us ready to get started here. Just to explain what I have, it's that Book class again about as simple as it gets, two NSStrings and an Integer. This Book class has no implementation we're speaking of, although I have added an init method just to begin with an author and title that have some basic information in those strings, I'll show you why in just a moment. There's not much else going on. In the AppDelegate, I have an NSMutableArray called allBooks that can hold multiple book objects, and I have created one listBooks IBAction method that's going to have just some simple code that will NSLog the contents of the array out so that we can see any difference between what we're seeing in the user interface and what's actually stored in the array.

And the last little piece of code worth exploring is in the implementation of AppDelegate. I have added an init method, and as soon as this class is being initialized, I'm creating this mutable array, and then I'm creating two instances of the Book class and adding them to the array. We have seen almost all of this code before. All I have currently on the interface file is one button that says List Book Objects. If I go ahead and run this, click that button, there will be no surprises. I just simply write out a very straightforward NSLog message for each object.

So I am going to stop that application. So at no point anywhere here is there any code that deals with user interface elements, writing any of this content out apart from that NSLog message. So let's start hooking things up. I am going to open up my Utilities Panel, and from the Object Library drop into Data Views where I'm going to drag on a Table view. This is the one that beforehand we had to hook up, create a data source and implement certain named methods to be able to provide data for every single row and every single column.

We're avoiding that whole approach and using binding this time around. Now here's the thing, this Table view does have a Binding section and Inspector, but I can't just bind it directly to that array in the AppDelegate. I want to use a different controller to be between this Table view object and the NSMutableArray of books, and here's how we're going to do it. From the Object Library, I'm going to select the section called Objects & Controllers under Cocoa, and here we have the Bindings compatible controller classes.

We have an array, so this Array Controller will work just fine. This is a non-visible object, so you drag it into the Dock rather than on to the interface. Remember, this is a controller, it's the middleman, so there are two connections that need to be made to this. I need to hook this controller to the actual NSMutableArray to the data, and then I'm going to hook the Table view

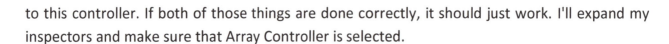

to this controller. If both of those things are done correctly, it should just work. I'll expand my inspectors and make sure that Array Controller is selected.

In the Bindings Inspector, what I'll see is that I have a section called Controller Content. This is an array controller, so not surprisingly it's looking for an array to handle. So it's asking, where is my Content Array, where is that? Well, that array is the allBooks array that's being stored right now in the AppDelegate class. So I am going to select to Bind to: App Delegate, and we're using the key idea out of key value coding. So self refers to the AppDelegate, but if I hit the dot, it should look into the properties that are available which includes the NSMutableArray of allBooks.

So our Array Controller is now pointed to our Array Model Data. Now, one thing I do want to do here is switch into the Attributes Inspector here because there are some attributes of this Array Controller that I want to change, too, which is I'm going to tell it exactly what that array contains. It starts off with this generic entry of an NSMutableDictionary, but no, I want that array to contain books. I know that is all that, that array contains. And that will make it easier to hook it up to our Table view.

So that's one side done, the controller is hooked to the model. Now, the controller needs to be hooked to the view. So I am going to select the Table view itself. Remember that whenever we drag on a Table view, what we get is a Table view inside a Scroll view. So, I can click again to select it, but if I want to be doubly sure, I will use the Dock here and expand to make sure I am selecting the actual Table view itself, not the Scroll view - Table view, and I'm going to bind this. So jump over into the Bindings Inspector, and it's asking okay, what's my content? And the main one I'm interested in here and Bindings is the table content.

It's asking, what am I binding to? Well, this time it's not to the AppDelegate, we are binding the Table view to the Array Controller. So that's correct here. We're saying Bind to the Array Controller, and that's all I actually need to do right now because the Array Controller contains those book objects. Now, you might be thinking, well, does that mean that everything works?No, nothing would happen yet because the objects that we have in that Array Controller could be significantly complex. We might not want to show everything on this Table view.

Chapter 8: Debugging and Troubleshooting

8.1 Using the Xcode Debugger

We have used a few simple troubleshooting techniques like using NSLog to send messages to the console, and we have talked about diagnosing the most common issues when hooking up your IBActions and IBOutlets correctly. But once you're past that, sometimes it's not quite so clear where the problem is, and you don't want to start writing dozens or hundreds of NSLog messages, so you want to be able to step through the code line by line as it executes. And we're going to do that now using the Xcode Debugger. This is just a brief introduction. If you have already been using the Debugger in iOS, I won't be telling you anything you don't know already.

So I have got a simple Cocoa application here called DebugStarter and looking at the MainMenu.xib file, I have got a button here conveniently titled Boom! and a blank label. Now that button calls some very straightforward code and a method called doSomething. It creates a couple of integers by calling some inner methods of this class, and then it divides one by the other, creates an NSString and spits that out to the label, some fairly simple stuff there. In fact, this code is all syntactically correct. It will compile if I hit Command+B, it'll go through and succeed, there is no problem there, but it is going to crash.

So let's go ahead and run it. I came over to the button, I click it. Now because we ran this directly from Xcode, we're jumping back into Xcode with all these great Debugger options appearing at the bottom of the screen here. Our application is still working. It's paused so we can view the inner workings of what's going on. So I have got the lower section showing up, if it's not you should be able to get to it from the view section here. And there's a problem, I can see immediately by this highlighted line, line 39 here, EXC_ARITHMETIC, we have some problem with Arithmetic. Okay, we'll get to that.

Now, over on the left-hand side what Xcode has jumped us to is the fifth navigator here which is the Debug navigator. It's showing us a stack trace, basically a list of where we are and how we got here, and it's the most recent at the top, this the main thread here. So it's telling us we're in the doSomething method of AppDelegate but we got here very gradually from NSApplication, NSApplicationMain and Start. Now towards the bottom I have this slider here, and if I actually start dragging that to the right and then to the left, what you'll actually see is different levels of the stack trace.

And that can sometimes give you a clue of how we got there, but right now most of these are really internal plots. We have the main method that called NSApplicationMain which hopefully remember from our lifecycle discussion, and a lot of the rest of the stuff going on here is basically being handled internally by NSApplicationMain. It's waiting for events. It's running, it's gotten a mouseDown, and it's kicked that mouseDown over to our doSomething method. So I don't need quite that level of information on my stack trace. I'll drag it to the middle. We just know we touch the button, it called our code, and there's a problem.

Now in the lower section here in the debug area I have the split between the variables view and the console. Console is telling me lldb here. We're using the low-level virtual machine debugger. Used to use gdb, but from Xcode 4.4 onwards we're using lldb. On the left-hand side I can see a list of Local Variables, and I can also use the dropdown here to move between the Local Variables which is what's shown automatically and All Variables, Registers, Globals, and Statics.

If I want to, and it's easier I can also mouse over the code to see the different values. Mousing over firstVal here tells me it's 10,000, mousing over the second one tells me it's zero. So there's the problem. We're trying to create an integer on line 39 by dividing 10,000 by 0, and that's an issue you can't do a divide by zero on a computing system, that is a problem. But let's imagine that it's a little bit challenging to figure out exactly where did these values come from.

SecondVal is zero that's a problem, but how did I get secondVal. So what I'm going to do is hover my mouse over the gutter section here, the gray bar beside the line numbers, that's if you have line numbering on. I'm going to click in here before the call to calculateFirstValue. When we set a breakpoint, we will break before this line is executed right at the start of it. Now because this program version isn't working, I'm just going to hit the Stop key here. So if I click in this gutter, I get this bright blue icon, which means it is a working breakpoint.

If I click again, it becomes somewhat dimmer, which means it's just not active right now. And you can kind of flip them back on and off. If I wanted to delete the breakpoint, I can just drag it off to the side and let go once I see the cloud icon. But I want it, so I'm going to put it back. If you actually start adding multiple breakpoints all up and down different parts of your code, and be aware that you are breaking before the line that the breakpoint is pointing to. If I had a lot, I can actually go to a different section of my navigators here, the Breakpoint navigator is the one that actually looks like the little blue marker points here, and it will give me another view of all the breakpoints in this project. What line they are on, what method they're in.

I can delete them from that view, or I can drag them off, and you can actually see them disappear as I do that. So I'm going to go ahead and run this with my one breakpoint just in the first line of the doSomething method. Our program is going to run normally because we haven't hit that code yet, it won't happen until I click the button. So I click it, we jump into the break mode. We're positioned before line 36. So if I hover over this, we're not going to get any kind of meaningful value here because I haven't run this line yet, this integer hasn't been initialized.

Down towards the middle section here, I have got the Debug bar that's going to allow me either just keep going until the next breakpoint, to Step Over the instruction, and that simply means execute it, but if it was calling a method don't go into the method, and then we can decide to step into the instruction. So in this case what that means is if I'm calling calculateFirstValue, which is a method in this current object, I'm going to hit the Step into, and we will actually jump into that method, and to calculateFirstValue, I can keep going, that returns 10,000, and that looks right.

What I should expect now when I am mousing over there is that value is 10000, looks good.Then I'm going to jump into the next one, which is calculateSecondValue. There is a bit more going on here. I'm creating an integer called zero. Integer b here is about to call the calculateFirstValue method again. I don't want to go into that, I saw it a moment ago, so what I will do instead is use the Step over version, which still means we called it, we did execute that line, but I just didn't want to go into that method and look at it. To prove we did execute it, I can actually see the b down here and our variable section is set to 10,000, or I could mouse over and see it that way.

So stepping forward, it looks we're in a fairly boring for loop here. And unfortunately this is going to go around 5000 times right now. I don't really want to click 5000 times, as it ticks down, so what I'm going to do is just step ahead and put a breakpoint before the return statement, and click the Play button to move ahead to that point. And looking at this, this appears to be the problem. And we're going to return zero from that. We're saying return a, and we should really have return the variable called b so there was actually some value.

Okay, so that was our problem. What I'm going to do is just stop. That was a little quick, so it thought it quit. Ignore that, I'm going to drag of my breakpoints and say that here I should be returning b, and in fact I don't need that integer a line. Ofcourse this was just a constructed way of causing a problem, but you get the idea. We go ahead and run it, and now our code is executing correctly, that 10,000 divided by 5000 is 2.

8.2 Creating An Exception Breakpoint

So you just saw how to use the debugger to analyze something like a divide by zero situation. There is actually a problem with using divide by zero, it's a little too obvious, not just to us but to the computer itself, because if you have a divide by zero issue, you will actually immediately break into this situation with the EXC_ARITHMETIC, because it's a very low level, what's called a signal that it is sending to the computer itself, we can't go any further than this. But some other cases, the program will actually try and continue on, and you won't immediately stop on the line that caused the problem, you actually break when Xcode figures out you can't go any further.

Now there is a couple of different ways that might manifest itself, but let me show you one of them. I'm just going to stop this running application and go and fix that divide by zero exception, which was just returning the variable called b instead of the variable called a, and then I'm going to go ahead and run this. I have created the project that has another error in it that's not necessarily quite so obvious, so I'm going to click Boom! And instead of jumping into a specific line with a nice green highlight, what we are getting down here are some error messages being sent out here to the console.

Now sometimes you can diagnose a message from that--I'm just going to widen this so we can see more about it. We have got mouse downs and sand effects, it's basically our call stack going on. And it does appear that we have got an index beyond bounds. But it's not telling me exactly what line I am looking at. Now, I could probably figure it out from this line here, because I've got a very simple application, but there is a better way of doing this. We can tell Xcode that we want to break immediately, as soon as any exception happens, as soon as anything detectable causes a problem.

This is the way we do it. I'm going to stop the app and just clear out my console, I don't need that right now. I'm going to jump into the breakpoints navigator, that's the one that looks like breakpoint symbol itself. Now I don't actually have any breakpoints right now, which is why nothing is showing up here, but I'm going to add one. And what I'm going to add is not a breakpoint for a particular line, but I'm going to add what's called a General exception breakpoint, telling Xcode I want to break if there's ever an Objective-C exception.

I do this by coming down to the plus button at the bottom of that breakpoint navigator. So again, I am on the second to last section here. And I click Add Exception Breakpoint. It gives me a pop-up window. What kind of exceptions do I want to break on? I'm going to say All of them. I could choose to do just Objective-C or C++. And Break as soon as the exception is Thrown. Optionally, I can click to add an Action, like play a sound or run a command, but I'm just going to leave everything as is click Done.

So I'll now break on All Exception, I'm going to go ahead and click Run, back to the app, click the button again. Now we immediately break, but we are breaking on the line that caused the problem. What's actually happening here is online 42 I am creating an array with three elements in it, which would be 0, 1, and 2, and then I'm trying to access what's at position 3, what's at index 3? Well, there is nothing there. So that's the actual problem here, and we are now breaking at the line that caused it, so it's much easier to diagnose.

8.3 Using Assertions

One useful technique for troubleshooting in Cocoa is using Assertions. Assertions help you find bugs earlier than you would otherwise. At a particular point in your code you can add Assertions. You assert something, you say at this point something should be true. A variable should be greater than 1,000, or a string should be a certain value, an object should be not nil.And if what I have asserted is false, that's a problem. So here I have a very simple method called doSomething being called by a button click. It itself is calling this complicatedCalculation method.

Now I might imagine there's an awful a lot going on here, but what I'm going to do is after our for loop, I'm really hoping that the variable foo is equal to 5000. In fact, that's what I want to assert. And I create assertions like this with a single call to NSAssert. It's a very simple line, it looks like a function call, and you can't think of it like that, but technically it's a macro, and that's very useful for a reason I'll explain in a moment. NSAssert takes two parameters, what are you asserting, what is the condition you're saying is true, phrased like a condition in an if statement.

So for me I'm going to say I expect the variable foo to be equal exactly to 5000, that's what I'm asserting. Then the second argument is the string. It's the message that should be logged if what I'm asserting is not true. So I'll just do this as an NSString here, the variable foo is the wrong value. So what happens is we're going to execute this code, we would come through thisfor statement, we'd hit line 24. And if what we see, what we have asserted is true, nothing happens, we simply move on.

However, if what we say what we have asserted is false, it will raise an exception, and it will log this message. And we could Ofcourse do this otherwise, fill our code with if statements, but this is a compact readable way to do it. So I'm going to go ahead and run the application.Click the button to Check Value, the value is 5000, nothing happens. Everything is as I said it should be, and we just continue. Quitting and going back into that, what I'll do is pretend we have made a slight change to the logic of our program. I'll just make a quick tweak to the forloop and run this again.

Now I click the button, and we instantly jump into the problem. I don't know if you saw here, but we're getting the messages being logged out here to the console, including that the variable foo is the wrong value. And this is important to understand, bear in mind when we use NSAsserts, this is not casual informational messages like you might do with NSLog. If an assertion fails, it throws an exception. It's a real problem. What you're saying is true, it should always be true, this should never fail, and it will cause your app to stop. And that's what we want here.

The reason that we do it as we're making these bugs more significant as early on as possible, and it's a great technique for developers. If we're going to fail, fail as soon as we can. Let us know about the problem early, so I can fix it, rather than return this value and pass it perhaps 10 levels deeper before we fail later on. Now, for example, I wanted to find out what the value of it was, we can actually call multiple different versions of Assert, there's NSAssert1,NSAssert2, and so on, just taking a different amount of format specifiers and parameters after the fact.

So if I wanted one parameter, I would use NSAssert1 and just change my string here so the variable foo is %i and pass that in. This time around when I run it, the message should just say: The variable foo is 4999, so very easy to add a very compact succinct way to do this.And one of the great things about this is that because NSAssert is technically a macro, here is one of the great things about it over, say, a function like NSLog.

We can pepper our code with these assertions, we can put them anywhere we think is useful, and while we're developing, they come in very handy, but it's pretty easy for us to add a small parameter to our Build Settings in Xcode.

Chapter 9: Distributing An Application

9.1 Archiving An Application For Distribution

So how do you get your Cocoa Application to somebody else? Let's say there are two situations here, first, the informal idea. You have created an app, even a simple one, and you just want to run it on another machine or even email it to a friend or colleague. And then there is the formal idea, you have worked for months on your application, and now you want to prepare it for distribution, either free or selling it yourself or Ofcourse, on the Mac App Store.Now we begin all of this the same way, by taking our project and archiving it, and when we're in our project in Xcode, we find the Archive option from the Product menu.

Now archiving might sound like an odd thing to do. If you think of archiving, it's something you do to put some old files in backup and forget about them. But what we're trying to do is formally bundle our application up at a point in time. An application archive for us is the application at a certain date in a certain state, so we may end up creating multiple archives at multiple times, but each time we intend to distribute an app formally or informally, we create an archive. So I'm going to select the Archive option from the Product menu. It creates an application archive and by default we'll open the Archive's Organizer.

This is actually not a new Window; it's the same organizer window you would use for Documentation or for source code repositories. And every time we archive the application, we'll have a new entry show up here. The application at a particular date and time. There is not much you can do on this window apart from add a Comment, perhaps I am creating a First try one for testing here. I can also choose to right- click this and Delete the Archive. If I choose to Show in the Finder, I'll see this Xcode archive file. This is actually a compressed file, we don't need to go into it, but you can find it there in the Finder.

Here is the two things I'm interested in are the buttons at the right-hand side to Validate and Distribute our application. What we should first do is Validate it. When we do this we have two choices: Validate for the Mac App Store, or for Direct Distribution. Now Validation doesn't do a tremendous amount, it's not validating your code just mainly doing some basic checks on the application. If you Validate for the Mac App Store, you're going to need to give it your Mac app credentials, and you need to have created an entry in iTunes Connect for this application, which means you have already got your Mac Dev account, you have gone through all the contracts arrangement setting up a company name and so on.

That's not necessary for us here, so what I'm going to do instead is Validate for Direct Distribution. This will perform a few simple checks. It's telling me that the archived application doesn't contain an icon. I haven't got a custom icon for this app yet. Well, I'm going to do that in a little while, so let's skip that for now just say Finish, and we'll see in the Status field here that we have Failed Validation. Doesn't really matter because I can choose to go ahead and distribute it anyway using the default application icon.

So I'll click Distribute, and again, we get a few different choices, do you want to Distribute for the Mac App Store, Export it with a Developer ID-signed or some other option? Now these options do often change in wording and in arrangement, they have changed between Xcode 4.2 and 4.3 and 4.4, so I don't guarantee that what you'll see will be exactly the same as what I'm seeing. Well, I'm going to go as informal as I can, and in this dropdown I have the option to Export as an Xcode Archive.

9.2 Working with Debug And Release Builds

So we need to archive our applications during the process of distributing them, but technically we could do a little more informally. You may have noticed that with something like a simple "Hello, World!" level application, when you build the application, it is already built as a Cocoa App. If you expand the Products folder in your project navigator, you'll actually find the application itself. I could right-click and choose to Show this in the Finder, and you could take this file just double-click it to run it, whether Xcode is open or not, or even copy it to another machine and run it there, but this really isn't the way to do it.

Because when we build, when we choose to run our application or hit Command+R to do that, what we're doing is running in debug mode, using a Debug Build. Your project has been compiled and linked together with symbolic debug information that's useful to us as developers but not to the end user. Might have things like the state of the breakpoints in the application.Now when we instead choose to Archive our application, we're using a Release Build instead of a Debug Build, and that does not include all the hooks into our code that the debugger needs.

Now it still does have some symbolic information which might help us diagnose crashes in a Released app, but it compiles and builds with a different set of options. So these Debug and release Builds are already set up in Xcode. They are already configured for a typical application. If I want to change anything about them, I can go to the Project settings and find the Build Settings for this just by clicking the top level icon with the project name in the Project Navigator. In this section we have Build Settings.

Now you'll actually find Build Settings under the both the Project selection and in the Target selection. A common question I get is what is the difference between the two? They both have Build Settings. Now for an example like this in a new Cocoa Application project, not really anydifference at all. We have one project, this entire project, this application that we're building that creates one target, the actual compiled application. In a more complicated project, you might have multiple targets, and each target could have slightly different build settings from the default project build settings.

Now particularly early on in your Cocoa career, you can leave everything here as is. If I decide to scroll through the Build Settings, and I can choose either the basic ones or click the All button here to see all of them, there are a lot of options. Again, most of them you don't really care about. What you'll find is that with a few, not many, there are different options for the Debug and Release. Coming down, for example, into the Preprocessing section, I have different Preprocess or Macros for Debug and Release, and one of the few things I might change, which I mentioned earlier on in the ebook is in the Preprocessor Directive section, and you can either scroll through this, you can also use the search filter button at the top here to filter down to anything that matches those words.

If I'm using Assertions, that I'm using that NSAssert call in my code, what I can do is make an entry here by double- clicking the Release section, click that plus button, and I will add in the NS_Block_Assertions entry. This written in uppercase with this particular format will strip out any of the NSAssert calls in my Release build. But one of the questions might be, how do Iknow what I'm using, how do I know if I'm using a Debug Build or a Release Build, where is that option? Well, that's already set up in Xcode 2, and it's in what's called a Scheme, a collection of settings for the different things.

9.3 Sandboxing An Application

Sandboxing is a technique Apple have introduced to help with security. Say you download a calculator app or buy one from the Mac Apps Store. Well, think about this, do you want that app to immediately have complete and total access to your file system, to the network, to your microphone and webcam, to the devices attached on your USB ports? Well, Ofcourse you don't, but by default that is the way that applications have worked in the past, they run with the privileges of the user who's running them. Sandboxing gets us away from this situation.

When we add Sandboxing, simply put, it means that applications are put in containers by the operating system, by OS X itself. Sandboxing limits what the application can do down to only what it needs to do, and it makes you as a developer say up front exactly what it is your app needs to do. And if attempts to do something else, that would be blocked and Sandboxing is important, this is now required, if you want to put your app in the Mac App Store. You have to say exactly where your application needs, there is a set of options, does it need the webcam? Does it need the microphone? Does it need access to the network? And you say exactly whether your app should be entitled to do any of these things, they're referred to as entitlements.

Chapter 10: Finishing Touches

10.1 Creating Full-Screen Apps

In OS 10.7 Lion, Apple introduced a standardized Full Screen mode for OS X, so apps can shift into taking over the entire screen. If I'm in Safari I just need to click this Full Screen icon at the top right of the Title Bar, and will take over the entire screen, even including the Apple menu. If I move my mouse up to the top I can make it comeback, so I can shift out of Full Screen mode, and I can still get to the Dock in most cases, but it allows us just to take over that space, Safari has it, Mail has it, even Xcode has the Full Screen option, so any app can choose to do this.

The first question Ofcourse is does it actually makes sense? There is two main reasons why you would want it. First will be creating a distraction- free reading or writing environment. For example, if I'm in Preview and reading a document, I can go full screen just to focus on the actual document that I'm taking a look at, and you'll find a quit a few writing tools also take over the full screen, even if they don't use the entire space to help you focus without being distracted by other applications And Ofcourse the other reason for it is when you have limited screen real estate and a lot going on in the application.

Say you're using Xcode on an 11-inch MacBook Air, being able to make that menu disappear and use every last available piece of screen can be very helpful, but on the other hand an application that you want to jump in and out of very quickly, like System Preferences, this would be a very poor choice for supporting full screen, and it doesn't support it. So it's not required, and it's not expected of everything, but it is very easy to implement if you choose to. Let's take a look. I have got a brand-new Cocoa application just to show that there is nothing that's been added here.

10.2 Creating Icons For OS X Applications

So far we have just been letting Xcode use the default application icon for our Cocoa Apps, that's the one that looks like this. You might see it in Xcode itself, but this icon is actually attached to the application itself, and unless we say otherwise, it's the one we are going to be using. Now creating icons for a Mac application is really two issues. There is the technical side, what do we need to do to make this work? And Ofcourse the creative side, what are all the things we could do with the icon design, things like color, perspective, should we use text and so on? Now for the creative side of things, I am going to point you mainly to the terrific section in the OS X Human Interface Guidelines, particularly the chapter on Icon Design.

There is a lot of great content here on using perspective and color and shadow and on other aspects many developers don't really think about, such as the different genres of icon that, in fact, Apple designs their icons differently based on the kind of application it is. Whether it's utility or a consumer app will drive different decisions regarding color and image.

But one more thing, it's not just five images, it's actually ten that are required because we must also provide duplicates of these at double resolution for a Retina display. So with the 512x512 icon, we also need that at 1024x1024 and so on, and Mac OS X will pick the right set of images for the correct device. And it's very important what you name these ten files because that's how OS X will pick the right image in the right situation.

And this is the format, the 512x512 pixel images should be icon_512x512.png. We have icon_256x256.png and so on. However, we can't just use this same format for the Retina display version because we'd actually end up with two icons of 512x512, so all the Retinadisplay icons end in @2x. But although the actual Retina icon might be 1024x1024, we would call it 512x512@2x.png, and this is the format that Apple use for the Retina artwork with the iPhone and iPad as well.

So these are the ten images that we need to create and the names of those images, and with those together we can start the process of getting them into our project. So in my Exercise Files folder, I actually have some icons that were created earlier. Just selecting them, I am going to use the spacebar to look a little bit at them. Here's the 16x16, same one at twice the resolution, they may go to 32, to 128, to 256, and to 512. Now I have created them slightly differently for each size, and you'll see why in a minute.

So here is what to do. Once you have got these images, you don't just drop them into Xcode. That would be too easy. In fact, the first step doesn't involve Xcode at all. First create a folder, and this folder can be anywhere. I am just going to put it on my Desktop, make a new folder here, and I will call it icon.iconset, and the name is important here. Now this is a stepping stone to creating a single file that will bundle all our images together. I have called that iconset. I am getting little confirmation message here, do I want to add the extension to the end of the name? Yes I do, so I will add that, and I am going to grab my ten images and just drag them into that iconset folder, and you might think, well what does that do? Well, this .iconset name Finder treats a little differently, so I am going to select that folder and then just hit the spacebar because what will happen is it gives us a quick look preview here that involves this little slider Bar at the bottom, and as I drag it smaller, we can actually see the different imagesappear at different sizes. That's why I try to make it a bit more obvious what's happening as we change the image, that we are actually picking the different files.

We are not just scaling it down, we are using a different image. But the next step is we need to take our .iconset folder and package all these images together into a single file which is called a .icns file. And Apple used to provide a separate program called icon composer to do this, butin Xcode 4.4 it was removed, and we use a command line tool instead.

Conclusion

Swift is a multi-paradigm, compiled programming language created by Apple Inc. for iOS, OS X, and watchOS development. Swift is designed to work with Apple's Cocoa and Cocoa Touch frameworks and the large body of existing Objective-C (Obj-C) code written for Apple products. Swift is intended to be more resilient to erroneous code ("safer") than Objective-C, and also more concise. It is built with the LLVM compiler framework included in Xcode 6, and uses the Objective-C runtime, allowing C, Objective-C, C++ and Swift code to run within a single program.

So we're reaching the end of this Ebook. What I wanted to do this ebook was as quickly as possible take you through the things you'll always need in every Cocoa application. Layouts and Controls, Target and Action, Delegation and MVC, application life cycle, data sources, key-value coding, and bindings and sandboxing, but Ofcourse, it gets deeper. And while we may have covered the things you'll need in every Cocoa app, we may not have covered the things you need in the one you want to build right now. You might need Core Data or iCloud or more on graphics and animation or working with audio and network communications. So the question is, well, what now? Now you got the basics, where do you go from here? And I think it's a great time to re-inspect the Mac Developer Center and the amount of content that is available here, because it's very easy to think of this as just reference, as your class reference libraries, but it's a lot more than that.

And particularly the documentation and the guides and the sample code are very usual. Of the two documents I think is essential for every new Cocoa developer to keep on hand the Mac Application Programming Guide and the OS X Human Interface Guidelines. Now, sometimes these can be a little tough to find, but if I go into the Developer Library section and select the Guides, we're going to find several hundred here. There's about 336 of them right now, but they can be grouped by topic. So if I click this to group them together, I'll find first--or at least prettyshortly--the general guides which includes things like Concepts in Objective-C, but also includes the Mac App Programming Guide. This is a great single document for detailing expected behavior of every OS X application.

Now it's a good one to keep on hand. These guides are provided both with HTML, and they also typically have a PDF link as well, if you want to download a copy. Now you can, Ofcourse, get to this documentation from within Xcode itself if you have the Organizer window open. Or if it's not, you can just get to from the Help > Documentation > API Reference. And then in the left-hand section, drill into the particular library for what you're working on, whether that's OS 10.7, or if you have OS 10.8 or even later.

Those themselves are split into the different categories. I could jump into the General section, and in here is where I should find the Mac App Programming Guide. What I can do here is right-click and add a Bookmark, that gives me the little bookmark section which can give me the favorite documentation that I have at the moment. So doing that, I am going to jump back in and then close down General, go into the User Experience section, and this is where we will find the Mac OS X Human Interface Guidelines, another really good one to always have bookmarked.

But whether you are using the Xcode Organizer or you're using the web site, you'll also find a selection of Sample Code. You can get that in the Developer Library, there is an entire Sample Code section. Do be aware that though there might be hundreds of sample projects, some of them are fairly old. In fact, the earliest ones go back to 2003, which doesn't necessarily mean they are all that useful for you in the current version of Xcode with current best practices and the current APIs and libraries.

I tend to prefer the ones that are from the last couple of years, so you can either drill through them on the web site, or you can get to them in the Xcode Organizer. You'll find this icon tends to represent some sample code here, so I might find say NSAlertTest. It allows me just to open the project, I can see that this last revision was in 2011, which isn't too bad. Directly open that from within the Organizer itself, and then I can take a look at some of the code that Apple would provide to illustrate certain concepts and ideas.

Cheatsheet

 Swift Cheat Sheet and Quick Reference

Class Implementation

```
class MyClass : OptionalSuperClass,
OptionalProtocol1, OptionalProtocol2 {

  var myProperty:String
  var myOptionalProperty:String?
  // More properties...

  // Only need override if subclassing
  override init() {
    myProperty = "Foo"
  }

  // More methods...
}
```

Methods

```
func doIt() -> Int {
  return 0
}
func doIt(a:Int) -> Int {
  return a
}
func doIt(a:Int, b:Int) -> Int {
  return a+b
}
```

Creating/Using an Instance

```
var a = MyClass()
a.myProperty
a.doIt()
a.doIt(1)
a.doIt(2, b:3)
```

Enums

```
enum CollisionType: Int {
  case Player = 1
  case Enemy = 2
}
var type = CollisionType.Player
```

Declaring Variables

```
var mutableDouble:Double = 1.0
mutableDouble = 2.0

let constantDouble:Double = 1.0
// constantDouble = 2.0 // error

var mutableInferredDouble = 1.0

var optionalDouble:Double? = nil
optionalDouble = 1.0
if let definiteDouble = optionalDouble {
  definiteDouble
}
```

Variable types	
Int	1, 2, 500, 10000
Float	1.5, 3.14, 578.234
Double	
Bool	true, false
String	"Kermit", "Gonzo", "Ms. Piggy"
ClassName	UIView, UIButton, etc

Control Flow

```
var condition = true
if condition {
} else {
}

var val = 5
switch val {
case 1:
  "foo"
case 2:
  "bar"
default:
  "baz"
}

// omits upper value, use ... to include
for i in 0..<3 {
}
```

String Quick Examples

```
var personOne = "Ray"
var personTwo = "Brian"
var combinedString = "\(personOne):
Hello, \(personTwo)!"
var tipString = "2499"
var tipInt = tipString.toInt()

extension Double {
  init (string: String) {
    self = Double(
      (string as NSString).doubleValue)
  }
}
tipString = "24.99"
var tip = Double(string:tipString)
```

Array Quick Examples

```
var person1 = "Ray"
var person2 = "Brian"
var array:[String] = [person1, person2]
array.append("Waldo")
for person in array {
  println("person: \(person)")
}
var waldo = array[2]
```

Dictionary Quick Examples

```
var dict:[String: String] = ["Frog":
  "Kermit", "Pig": "Ms. Piggy",
  "Weirdo": "Gonzo" ]
dict["Weirdo"] = "Felipe"
dict["Frog"] = nil // delete frog
for (type, muppet) in dict {
  println("type: \(type), muppet:
\(muppet)")
}
```

Source: raywenderlich.com. Visit for more iOS resources and tutorials!